Praise for *My Canada Includes Foie Gras*

"If you care deeply about dining … get this book."

—*National Post*

"*My Canada Includes Foie Gras* is a great addition to the Canadian gourmand library. Richler takes us on a passionate gastronomic journey across the country."

—Daniel Boulud, Restaurant Daniel, NYC

"The combination of [Richler's] knowledge and experience with his expressive writing style makes *My Canada Includes Foie Gras* a reader's treat … Sumptuously written and clearly showing his love of good food, this collection of Canadian cooking perspectives is sure to send you to the fridge looking for a decadent midnight snack."

—*Winnipeg Free Press*

"Richler's food-centric tales relate in rich detail a life full of adventure and belly-bloating joy. Through his patriotic curiosity and thoughtful research, we learn the intricacies of Canada's flavourful but often overlooked culinary history. As a smoked meat deprived ex-pat, *My Canada Includes Foie Gras* made me long for the smells, sounds and tastes of my homeland."

—Gail Simmons, bestselling author of
Talking With My Mouth Full

"Witnessed in Canada's most accomplished kitchens—including Richler's own—this is the gourmets' gospel, last testament of the golden age of eating. Read it when you're very, very hungry."

—James Chatto, award-winning
food writer and restaurant critic

"All you need is great results which ... Richler delivers. [His] culinary life and his rule-bending intimacy with his subjects has clearly led to a solid bank of knowledge about food preparation, which he shares." —*Toronto Star*

"A wonderful and highly personal account of what's good to eat in Canada, where to find it and how to cook it. His tales of the gastronomic habits and eccentricities of the Richler family are fascinating. Richler knows and has worked with the top chefs in the country. He is highly knowledgeable, acutely discriminating, loves controversy and takes no prisoners. A must-read for all who care about what goes into their stomach."

—Sondra Gotlieb, journalist and award-winning novelist

PENGUIN

MY CANADA INCLUDES FOIE GRAS

JACOB RICHLER writes regularly on food and other topics for *Maclean's* and several other publications. He has won two National Magazine Awards. Richler is well-known for his food writing and for his books with Chef Susur Lee (*Susur: A Culinary Life)* and Mark McEwan (*Great Food at Home* and *Rustic Italian).*

Visit his website at jacobrichler.com.

MY CANADA INCLUDES

{ A CULINARY LIFE }

JACOB RICHLER

PENGUIN

an imprint of Penguin Canada Books Inc., a Penguin Random House Company

Published by the Penguin Group
Penguin Canada Books Inc., 90 Eglinton Avenue East, Suite 700, Toronto, Ontario, Canada M4P 2Y3

Penguin Group (USA) LLC, 375 Hudson Street, New York, New York 10014, U.S.A.
Penguin Books Ltd, 80 Strand, London WC2R 0RL, England
Penguin Ireland, 25 St Stephen's Green, Dublin 2, Ireland (a division of Penguin Books Ltd)
Penguin Group (Australia), 707 Collins Street, Melbourne, Victoria 3008, Australia (a division of Pearson Australia Group Pty Ltd)
Penguin Books India Pvt Ltd, 11 Community Centre, Panchsheel Park, New Delhi – 110 017, India
Penguin Group (NZ), 67 Apollo Drive, Rosedale, Auckland 0632, New Zealand
(a division of Pearson New Zealand Ltd)
Penguin Books (South Africa) (Pty) Ltd, 24 Sturdee Avenue, Rosebank, Johannesburg 2196, South Africa

Penguin Books Ltd, Registered Offices: 80 Strand, London WC2R 0RL, England

First published in Viking hardcover by Penguin Canada Books Inc., 2012
Published in this edition, 2014

1 2 3 4 5 6 7 8 9 10 (WEB)

Copyright © Jacob Richler, 2012

Portions of this work were previously published in slightly different form in the *National Post* and *Maclean's*.

Manufactured in Canada.

LIBRARY AND ARCHIVES CANADA CATALOGUING IN PUBLICATION

Richler, Jacob, author
My Canada includes foie gras : a culinary life / Jacob Richler.

Includes index.

Originally published: Toronto : Viking, 2012.

ISBN 978-0-14-318085-2 (pbk.)

1. Richler, Jacob—Travel--Canada. 2. Food writers—Travel—Canada. 3. Food habits—Canada.
4. Cooking, Canadian. 5. Cooks—Canada—Anecdotes. 6. Canada—Description and travel. I. Title.

TX649.R53A3 2014   641.092   C2014-900461-3

Visit the Penguin Canada website at **www.penguin.ca**

Special and corporate bulk purchase rates available; please see
www.penguin.ca/corporatesales or call 1-800-810-3104, ext. 2477.

For my mother, who got me started
on the culinary path (and a few others),
And for Lisa, because

CONTENTS

INTRODUCTION

One summer afternoon in 2006 I dropped by a restaurant called Bistro and Bakery Thuet, in downtown Toronto, entering as was my habit through its back door directly into the kitchen. I had arrived just in time to spot another unexpected visitor, Franco Prevedello, plucking a biscuit from a large unattended batch cooling on a baking sheet, and taking a large bite. On the surface of it there was nothing wrong with Prevedello helping himself. He had been a driving force in the Toronto restaurant scene for decades, was the signatory for the lease on the bistro's premises, and enjoyed a business relationship with its chef and co-owner, Marc Thuet, that dated back to the eighties, when Prevedello had employed him at his Centro Grill & Wine Bar on Yonge Street. The problem had to do with something else.

"Franco!" I called out. "Stop! Those are *dog* biscuits!"

Prevedello stopped chewing and looked at me. And then after a pause flashed his trademark mischievous smile from beneath his bushy moustache, shrugged, and popped the rest of it in his mouth.

"They're good!" he said.

My dog Bonko certainly thought so. For only the day before, when I was running errands with him, I had stopped for some bread at the bistro and chef Thuet had given me a bag of the biscuits. En route home, when I parked to collect something else on my list, I left the biscuits in the car with Bonko, who was napping on the back seat, with an air of sweet innocence about him. By the time I returned he was instead sitting upfront, looked charged, and sheepish. The aroma of the biscuits had apparently awoken him. Then he had managed something he had never even attempted before, and somehow extracted them from the driver's door side-pouch. He ate all of them, right down to the last crumb, and then chewed the paper bag to bits, too, for good measure.

You might think that a dog treat that acts like smelling salts on a mutt with canine narcolepsy, like mine, and also pleases the palate of a top restaurateur must be something out of the ordinary. It was. This is the thing: just before he baked them, chef Thuet had churned the raw dough with a good dose of Quebec's finest Grade A foie gras.

The initiative did not arise out of the blue. That year marked heady days for the anti–foie gras movement. Stateside, affirmative duck action was gaining the upper hand. It had already been two years since Governor Schwarzenegger of California had assertively demonstrated that he was capable of far greater empathy for ducks than, say, his wife, by signing into law an act that would ban both foie gras production and consumption in the state by mid-2012.

Closer to home, Chicago city council had just voted to ban foie gras from all retail stores and restaurant tables within its city limits—an American first (although the ban would be repealed two years later). And the unofficial figurehead for that particular movement was none other that the city's best-known and most accomplished chef, Charlie Trotter, who for "ethical reasons" had stopped serving foie gras in his restaurants back in 2002. The ten-times James Beard award winner was a virtuoso in the kitchen who had already proved singularly influential in driving trends, from the blind tasting menu to raw food. Trotter also happens to be a well-spoken and thoughtful man. Amongst chefs and the dining public, his credibility with regards to the rights of animals and livestock was nearly unimpeachable.

But chef Thuet did not see it that way. For he hails from Alsace, where foie gras is neither contentious product nor luxury item—but rather, a staple. It was there, in Strasbourg in 1780, that some four and a half millennia after the ancient Egyptians started force-feeding geese, chef Jean-Pierre Clause devised the method for turning its resultingly bloated liver into a silken terrine, and foie gras finally attained its apotheosis. "The goose is nothing," Charles Gérard wrote in *L'Ancienne Alsace à table* in 1862. "But man has made of it an instrument for the output of a marvellous product, a kind of living hothouse in which there grows the supreme fruit of gastronomy."

Foie gras has been a cornerstone of Alsatian cuisine for centuries. Which is why it is rumoured that baby chef Thuet was weaned on the stuff mashed up on a little spoon. Some people even say that as an infant, he tumbled into a large, warm, and unset terrine of the stuff and—like Obelix and the cauldron of magic potion—derived from the dunking a secret culinary strength. Either way, he is one of the few chefs I know who has actually walked into a goose or duck pen with a feeding tube in one hand and a sack of grain in the other—and been mobbed by the hungry, expectant birds.

"They fucking love it!" he assured me, of *le gavage*.

Maybe, but perhaps not; all that is absolutely certain to me is that out there in the wilds beyond the holding pen, nature promises innumerable fates far worse than a spot of force-feeding. The thing about ducks and geese is that when left to their own devices, they will twice a year behave as do all migratory birds prior to the big annual trip and gorge themselves silly like a crowd of Americans at an all-you-can-eat buffet in Las Vegas. The biannual binge leaves their livers naturally engorged. Which is why all those millennia ago hunters and cooks noticed that duck and goose livers were fatter and tasted better during their period of pre-migratory feasting. And the reason that they first put their minds to the simple task of replicating those circumstances all year round. In other words, those greedy ducks and geese brought this upon themselves.

So when word spread in the summer of 2006 that Charlie Trotter was coming to town to be a guest chef at Susur Lee's flagship restaurant, Susur, which just happened to be situated on King Street West, right alongside Bistro and Bakery Thuet, chef Thuet got rather agitated. He did not want to seek out a confrontation, but neither could he let it pass unaddressed. Which is when he suddenly remembered having heard that Charlie Trotter had a dog—and decided to bake him a batch of special foie-gras-laced treats.

When Trotter cancelled the engagement it was a great day for Bonko. Some of the biscuits ended up in gift bags at the Toronto International Film Festival. Others went to other spoiled hounds around town whose parents were Thuet regulars and were thus invited to partake of the foie gras biscuit leftovers. "Those dogs see me, they still wag their tales like crazy," Thuet maintained years later.

That fall I moved into a house on a park in Cabbagetown, one of Toronto's oldest neighbourhoods. And one day, returning home after a pleasantly long lunch, I disembarked from the cab alongside a Toyota Prius hybrid with a giant sticker on one door bearing the message "Say No to Foie Gras." This obnoxious intrusion into an otherwise pleasant day was irritating, but I saw no driver about to confront, and by the time I got to my front door I had forgotten all about it. Until I opened my refrigerator to fetch a bottle of mineral water—and in my peripheral vision, a tin on one of the shelves on the door started dancing about, exclaiming in a speech bubble in my mind's eye, "Pick me, pick me!"

It was a can of Hungarian foie gras d'oie given to me by my friend Arpi Magyar, a superb chef to whom I am forever indebted for letting me in on his secret of the seared-foie-gras-and-bacon breakfast sandwich. It was clear what I had to do: I got a knife from the drawer, cut the label from the can, popped outside, and stuck it under the windscreen wiper of the offending Prius. And then I went back home to work and forgot all about it.

Until a few hours later, when I was heading out with Bonko

for an afternoon walk, and opened my front door to find a large envelope on my stoop. It was addressed to me by hand. In fact it said, "Jacob—you know better!" Inside was a stack of papers on the evils of foie gras. I looked around, combed the park, and peered down the street. Nobody. And no Prius, either.

In these modern times when more and more of us live in complete urban detachment from the pastoral life, oblivious to the workings of the farms that deliver food to our plates, it is increasingly inevitable that every good neighbourhood will feature at least an incipient pocket of crusading vegetarians—or self-hating carnivores, as I see them. But the news that there was a crazed ducks' rights activist living close enough to me to know my name and address and to track my movements was nonetheless disturbing. Had they been rummaging through my recycling bin for spent foie gras jars? Did they know Bonko had a problem, too—and that his second-favourite treat was kangaroo strips?

Weeks passed before I saw the Prius again. When it drove slowly by, and then turned up a dead-end street perpendicular to mine, I followed at a discreet distance. The driver parked the car in a driveway at the top of the street. I hung about behind a nearby tree, and waited and watched. And out stepped the Giller Prize–nominated author of *Mr. Sandman* and *The White Bone*, Barbara Gowdy.

I suppose like a good neighbour I should have invited her over for dinner sometime. But I would not have known what to serve. I keep a healthy kitchen. You will find nothing processed here, not even sliced bread. The stocks are all made in-house. The only thing I take out of a can each week is San Marzano tomatoes and the only frozen foods in my freezer were cooked and put there by me. But while ever since Mark Bittman published *Food Matters: A Guide to Conscious Eating*, I have made a stab at eating a vegetarian dinner once a week, I remain an omnivore, without dilemma. When I buy lamb I buy a whole one, head and offal attached. Not all of the fish I eat is endorsed by Ocean Wise. And more to the point, to a lover of living ducks on a diet, my place would seem like a bloody film set from the *Saw* franchise.

My basement fridge always boasts an assortment of vacuum-packed confits for emergencies—Pekin for light lunches, and moulards for proper dinners. There are backup lobes of raw Grade A foie gras in the freezer, and jarred terrines in the fridge. I usually have a batch of vacuum-packed magrets aging in the meat drawer. And I always have jarred duck gizzard confit on hand for a quick luncheon salad with frisée and shallot vinaigrette. You will not find a customer loyalty card for Starbucks or Tim Hortons in my wallet, but I do have one for the Brome Lake Duck store in Knowlton, Quebec, where every tenth duck product purchase means you get to pick any item for free.

My children, Max and Simone, are showing every sign of carrying on this appreciation of the world's first domesticated bird (thank you, China). It was some years ago—when they were aged about five and six—that I took them down to a Chinese restaurant called Pearl Harbourfront, on Toronto waterfront, for a ceremonial Sunday treat of their first Peking duck. The restaurant is Cantonese, and so their duck is not authentic, but they do a decent job all the same. But when I first spotted the waiter wheeling a trolley laden with the bird and its fixings our way, my customarily eager anticipation was tempered by the observation that the beautifully bronzed bird was still sporting its head. Would Simone now notice the obvious anatomical connection between lunch and the little stuffed fuzzy duck with which she liked to spend the night? My treat looked poised to backfire.

But when the waiter waved the platter around for its customary pre-carving parade lap, neither child noticed anything disturbing. Their interest was piqued when the busboys started setting up our table with little plates of hoisin, scallions, and a steamer basket full of pancakes. And they watched enraptured as our waiter carefully carved the duck into slices of moist breast topped with a little fat and a good shard of bronze glazed skin. He arranged them as prettily as he could manage on a large oval platter. Then he chopped the head off the carcass and with a flourish placed it beak outwards at one end of the platter.

Uh-oh, I thought. And then, as if he had planned it that way all along, the waiter lifted the platter from the trolley and placed it at the centre of our table, in such a way that the duck's head was pointing directly at my daughter like a dart, its roasted bill dangling over the edge of the platter and straying into her place setting. Upper and lower mandibles were parted, revealing a shrivelled black tongue within. There was no way she was going to eat this bird, I thought. Far more likely that she would very shortly burst into tears.

At which point Simone picked up a chopstick, poked the head above the beak, right between the eyes, and said, "What's up, duck?"

~ 1 ~

HOME

On Labour Day weekend, 2011, my mother, Florence, my brothers, Daniel and Noah, my sisters, Emma and Martha, and I gathered at our old family cottage on Lake Memphremagog in the Eastern Townships, near Montreal, for a bittersweet reunion. My father, Mordecai, had died ten years previous. Not long afterwards my mother lost her sight—and even before that sad day, she could not drive, and was far too scared of mice or the sound of twigs snapping in the woods at night to ever stay in that house alone. Meanwhile, it had been more than fifteen years since any of the rest of us had lived within six hundred kilometres of the place. The time had come to sell and pack up.

We had moved in on Canada Day weekend, 1974—the summer in which Duddy Kravitz made it to the silver screen, and his zeyda was spreading the word that "a man without land is nobody." As it happened, my father's new land was a very modest parcel of a couple of acres. It was the particular vantage that had so tidily manifested his boyhood dream of owning his own place on a lake in the Quebec countryside. In the peace and quiet of that private hilltop overlooking the length of Sergeant's Bay, he would write his best books, and enjoy much treasured, uninterrupted reading time. And between those two habits he had accumulated many thousands of volumes that were scattered all over the house. My mother had a library, too. We had all done our share of accumulating, and then collectively used the place as a free storage depot for years after we had moved far away. Now it all had to go. My father's vast library was to be packed up and dispatched to his new archives at Concordia University (his alma mater, if you still call it that when you drop out). Much of the rest of it had to be shipped to our various houses in Montreal, Toronto, Digby Neck (Nova Scotia), and London (U.K.). And a whole lot more would have to be given away or thrown out. The worst part of it all was that somehow—whether by draft or foolish volunteerism, I can no longer recall—I had ended up as principal liaison with the moving company that would be taking care of it all. So it was that a few months earlier, in an attempt to diminish the scale of the inevitable horror of that fateful weekend, I had tried to get started on the organizational front by asking all my siblings to send along lists of what they wanted to take away with them.

Reality has a nasty way of intruding on some otherwise excellent plans. There was, for example, much interest in my father's regulation-size snooker table—until everyone remembered that they were unequipped with a spare, empty room of the required minimum dimensions (eighteen by twenty-four feet, seriously). And for my part I had long coveted our venerable four-oven AGA cooker, which my father had had installed as part of a kitchen renovation a quarter-century before, to help my mother miss England less and cook for him more.

The AGA is the quintessentially English stove. It is unapologetically old-fashioned, identical in appearance and principle both to the latest models available in your local showroom and to the earliest museum-piece editions from the 1920s. If it were a car, it would be a Morgan (lovely to look at, shockingly dated, but still a surprisingly good idea). They are manufactured more or less by hand in Coalbrookdale, Shropshire, where the process begins at a three-hundred-year-old foundry that was once the cradle of the Industrial Revolution—the very place where iron had its seminal rendezvous with coke. Cast iron is the key to the AGA's design. Each of its four ovens is encased in a sleeve of the stuff cast to a different thickness. The gauge of that sleeve helps define the level of heat within it. For the AGA has just one central heat source, which rages constantly. In other words, your four-oven AGA cooker packs a full set of permanently preheated ovens—one each for roasting, baking, simmering, and warming. This is not just convenient but a culinary virtue, for the heat radiates remarkably evenly from those iron walls, and it does so without any drying internal airflow. The AGA is an almost uniquely magnificent vehicle for executing the Sunday roast, just as its central surface heat plate is ideally suited to preparing risotto—and the list goes on.

Alas, so do the fuel costs, for that relentlessly firing heat source obviously consumes a lot of gas. While that gave me pause, there was something else, far worse. An AGA is designed to spill heat into the room and house around it. This is very handy in winter—especially in poorly insulated, damp English homes. But even there, it is a burden in summertime—which is why most English people turn theirs off for the season, and turn instead to their backup set of ovens and hobs. Even I had to admit that this made the AGA singularly ill suited for my own family's summer-only, sunlight-flooded Ontario cottage—where, to come clean, it would hardly have fit anyway. And our city house was no better suited to the thing, for the old AGA was gas powered, and these models (unlike newer electric editions) can be installed against outside walls only—and not shared ones, like the one that runs behind my Toronto kitchen. So that was that. Just like the snooker table, the six-hundred-kilogram AGA would be staying put.

Fortunately my mother's big country kitchen featured a number of other attractions that were far easier to pack. Near the top of my list was something of the same colour and country of origin as the AGA, but an older vintage, and an altogether more modest price bracket: her lovely old black porcelain pie bird, its up-stretched yellow beak a vent for steam. More precious still was a well-worn and seemingly indestructible plate from Schwartz's delicatessen on the Main—just the right size for two medium-fats-on-rye—which sometime in the late eighties, in a rare moment of teenage inspiration, I had given to my father for Christmas, with a gift certificate taped to it that was exchangeable for one whole smoked meat brisket (eight pounds, maximum). I strongly doubt that my father ever remembered to exchange the coupon—but he did treasure that plate. In fact for the rest of his days in that house, save for those rare occasions when we had company, he ate his solitary lunch from it every day. Same plate, same lunch. For the first course, one or two thickly sliced Quebec beefsteak tomatoes.

Then—no need to rinse—a pair of *saucisses de Strasbourg*. The veal wieners were invariably burst open, their casing split and toughened from a stint in the AGA's roasting oven (ill advised, yes, but faster than poaching), and plated, for balance, with a couple of hunks of schmaltz herring and a large dipping pool of Heinz Chili Sauce.

My mother preferred a loftier set of comfort foods, and her long quest to get them right was embodied in my principal treasure haul from the family cottage: her cookbook library. She had started buying them in 1947, shortly after quitting Montreal for London. Between the food books she acquired there, and the Canadian and American editions that followed our family's return to Canada in 1972, there were now by my count some eight metres' worth of volumes dispersed among our country kitchen's rustic pine shelves. I had little time to sort through them and decide which to pack and which to discard. And while separating quirk and quality from undesirables is usually easy when you know the subject well, it quickly proved difficult to stay focused on the job at hand and not get distracted by some of the finds. There were so many treasures in the heap. Take, for example, her 1948 printing of the *Larousse Gastronomique*, which amongst innumerable other quirks, includes a most eccentric entry for rhubarb, containing this statement: *"La feuille peut se manger cuite comme les épinards."* ("You may prepare and eat the leaves just as you would spinach.") "Never," my mother had written in pencil in the margin long ago, "poisonous." And indeed, while by most estimates it would require an impractical five-pound serving to pack a fatal dose of the rhubarb leaf's toxic oxalic acid, there remains a lot of unpleasant middle ground to be wary of between a nice dinner and untimely death.

Like so many of her volumes, the *Larousse* bears testimony to how much cooking has changed over the years—and no entry in that old culinary encyclopedia illustrates this more readily than that for "oeuf." You may have heard the old story that a chef's hat—or toque—traditionally contained one hundred starched pleats (forty-eight is now more typical) as a symbol of the one hundred different ways in which any self-respecting chef should be able to prepare an egg. If you have, but found the story implausible, or even impossible, then you need to spend a little time with an old *Larousse*. Specifically, an edition printed before the shameful 1970s, when the American Heart Association demonized the egg on the basis of its improperly analyzed cholesterol content, and caused the once unassailable pillar of French gastronomy to plummet in public favour. From *Oeufs à l'africaine* (couscous, eggplant, bell pepper, tomato sauce) through *Oeufs Cardinal* (pastry shell, lobster with béchamel, *sauce cardinale*, and shaved truffle!) through to the final entry of *Omelette au sucre* (sugar, zest of mandarin orange), the egg section of the old *Larousse* spans twenty pages and well over five hundred different recipes. The American egg-white omelette is not among them.

What we choose to cook—and the way we elect to cook it—changes all the time. Presentation and plating styles date as fast as last year's hemlines. Culinary ideas that are revolutionary when launched tend to either fall by the wayside, justifiably forgotten, or get so thoroughly absorbed into the mainstream that we soon stop thinking of them as something that had ever been new. Either way, years on and out of context, books of once significant recipes have a way of appearing irrelevant. It was impossible to avoid thinking about this as I pulled books from the shelves authored by the celebrity chefs of an earlier era. Like *Cuisine Minceur* by Michel Guérard, which spawned a movement but today just reads like a necessary and overdue step in the flour, butter, and cream–shedding evolution of French sauces (and a stage unnecessary to revisit). *The Cuisine of Frédy Girardet* contains many dishes with more enduring appeal. But the fuss generated by his cooking (the Gault-Millau guide proclaimed him "a genius") is difficult to reconcile with the stark simplicity of his recipes—like *Salade de ris de veau au pois gourmands*, which is nothing but a sauté of sweetbreads and snow peas with a few drops of walnut oil and a squeeze of lime. Next I pulled from the shelf a 1978 edition of *The Nouvelle Cuisine of Jean & Pierre Troisgros* and came face to face with the back-cover photograph of their vegetable terrine "*olympe*," a ham mousse set with artichokes and carrots served in a pool of cold tomato sauce and topped with a scattering of pallid green beans. It looks very horrible. But the book redeems itself slightly with its recipe for the 1966 dish that was said to have single-handedly earned the Maison Troisgros its third Michelin star: *Saumon à l'oseille*—escalope of salmon flash-seared in a dry pan and then served on top—rather than under—its sorrel cream sauce. Uneventful now, but revolutionary then: in fact every piece of succulent, lightly seared fish you have eaten since owes a little something to that dish. And the same thing goes for your next serving of fish or poultry that has delicious crispy skin—even though it came with sauce—because someone thought to put the liquid on the plate first and the protein second. When chefs do something new just right like that, it gets around to other good restaurants fast. And soon enough it enters mainstream cooking, and we forget all about the origins. It happens all the time—even with home cooking.

Picture, for example, the following scene taken from my mother's same country kitchen several years earlier. In the years after my father died it was my custom to take my wife and family on vacation to Memphremagog each August, always pausing in Montreal en route from Toronto to collect my mother, who enjoyed being part of it. That is the cast, it is late afternoon, and as usual at this time I am to be found in the kitchen. The workspace is spacious, and equipped with plenty of windows and skylights to let the sunshine in. There is a central island and peripheral counters too, for those inclined to help, along with plenty of seating for those who are not. And on this particular occasion it was as usual something of a split, with a lot of drinks being poured and re-poured, and just about everyone ignoring my mother Florence's No Smoking signs, even though she was there in the midst of it—just as my father had always done. Meanwhile (as we got by without a summer-only backup set of ovens and hobs), the AGA cooker was going strong, billowing unwanted heat around the room. All the same, it had a welcome way of somehow using the silent assertion of its six-hundred-kilogram heft to ground the chaos around it in the shared purpose of dinner.

A casual dinner for eight, this time. And on the menu was a dish of my mother's that had been one of my father's favourites: a lobster pasta with a tomato cream sauce, enriched with an extensive mirepoix of vegetables, and fragrant with paprika and thyme. It was also a dish that in his estimation his hard work more than hers put on the table. Not because he paid for the lobster, but rather because he boiled them and shelled them—and what a spectacle that was. He was not at ease in the kitchen—or at least, he shouldn't have been—and for him processing three or four lobsters was a multi-cigar-and-whisky job. Cleavers, hammers, screwdrivers, and whatever other tools happened to be on hand somehow got involved. There was much huffing and puffing, and the bits of shell and muck and guts flew absolutely everywhere. The cleanup (not his thing) was arduous. Invariably all the same, many weeks and sometime months after this Jew vs. crustacean showdown, someone would reach up to a high shelf to retrieve an obscure cookbook or a seldom-used piece of cooking equipment and a dried-up lobster leg or hunk of shell would tumble down and bounce, rattling, across the quarry-tile floor, and everyone in the kitchen would stare at it silently where it came to rest, thinking, "How the hell did that get up there?"—and slowly, the horror would come back.

I was trying to do the job with a little less mess, and quite successfully. I was also preparing the dish *my* way. For in the years when my mother made the dish, the prevailing culinary wisdom had it that even when preparing lobster for the first phase of a dish where it would later be cooked again—say, for lobster Thermidor or soufflé—it should be cooked very nearly to completion. So it was with her lobster pasta. But my preference had long been to only lightly par-cook it, as one would in preparation for making butter-poached lobster, and then let the meat finish cooking in the sauce itself. The second change was a new one—one ingredient dropped and a fresh one inserted—and this was not of my doing but rather at the vociferous instruction of a real chef. And as it was my mother who had originally taught me the dish, and all who know her would describe her as, well, rather sensitive, it was to me obvious that it would be best all around if I kept news of both of these possible improvements to her dish to myself. So I did not mention it as I cooked, or when I toasted her at the table just before we all tucked in. But looking down the table at her as she took her first bite, I noticed a mildly perplexed expression on her face, and it remained there, gaining concentration, as she took another small taste, and then another.

"You've changed something," she said.

"Well, yes," I said, and fearing the worst, quickly added, "It wasn't my idea—it was Marc Thuet's!"

She has met the Alsatian chef with me many times in Toronto—first during his stint at Easy & The Fifth, on Richmond Street, and later at his own restaurant, on King Street West, then called Bistro and Bakery Thuet. Whether or not like me she considered him to share sensibilities with Fernand Point—or just a physique—we had never precisely discussed; but I knew her for a fact to be a great admirer of his cooking, as well as of his rather astonishingly unselfconscious nature. So I went ahead and told her the story.

The week before, I had been enjoying a reinvigorating

post-lunch cognac at the bar at Bistro Thuet when Marc sat down alongside to join me. The customary topic of discussion—food—soon turned to what I would be eating at the cottage on vacation the following week. I told him about the local supermarket—Métro Plouffes—fifteen minutes up the road in Magog (population twenty-five thousand), which stocks an exceptional selection of items that you would have to special order at even the finest stores in Toronto (population six million): horsemeat, cold-smoked venison loin, whole lobes of foie gras, fresh local (Brome Lake) ducklings, dozens of different terrines and pâtés, you name it. I got started on the fish counter and its Matane shrimp and three kinds of sea bream—and that's when he began questioning me rather forcefully about how exactly I made my lobster pasta.

" … so you sweat the onions, garlic, carrot, celery, red and green bell peppers—"

"FUCKING BELL PEPPERS? YOU PUT FUCKING *BELL PEPPERS* IN YOUR FUCKING LOBSTER PASTA?! YOU FUCKING IDIOT!!!" He extinguished the horrible menthol cigarette he was smoking directly in his freshly emptied can of Diet Coke and glowered at me. Staff and customers alike who knew him and were accustomed to his vigorous language nonetheless stared at us, but he continued undeterred. "YOU DON'T PUT FUCKING BELL PEPPERS IN LOBSTER PASTA, YOU IDIOT! YOU PUT FUCKING FENNEL!!"

So that was that: out with mirepoix of red and green bell peppers and in with the half bulb of fennel. My mother enjoyed the story. But she did not say what she thought of the dish, not until many hours later, when, in the early hours of the morning, matters tableside were devolving some and she had announced that it was time to retire. I walked her to her room, shut her door and was heading back to the dining room when she opened it again and called after me.

"Oh, Jake?"

"Yes."

"About the fennel."

"Yes?"

"I think Marc's fucking right!"

My mother was then seventy-eight. It was the first time I had ever heard her use the word.

Back in my mother's kitchen, I was still packing up books—and cheerfully, because I had finally located her 1973 first edition of *The White Elephant Cookbook*, an anthology of recipes culled from some of the many celebrities who in the 1960s and '70s gathered at the celebrated White Elephant club on Curzon Street, in Mayfair. To come clean, it is the nature of that old clientele far more than their recipes that provides the value of the book. Their explanatory notes generally endure better than the recipes that follow. For example, the late John Mortimer (author of *Rumpole of the Bailey*) introduces his fish pie recipe by proclaiming British food the very best in the world. (When he made his case in 1972, the same might well have been said about British weather.) Mortimer's recipe proceeds without a single measurement ("I

Lobster Pasta with Fucking Fennel

Florence Richler

Serves 6

2 lobsters, about 1-3/4 lb (790 g) each
3 tbsp (45 mL) olive oil
1 small Spanish onion, minced
2 cloves garlic, minced
1 stalk celery, peeled and minced
1 carrot, minced
1/2 fennel bulb, minced
2 tsp (10 mL) thyme leaves, chopped
2 cans (28 oz/796 mL each) San Marzano tomatoes, milled
2 tsp (10 mL) sweet paprika
Salt and pepper
1-1/2 cups (375 mL) 35% cream
Fettuccine (or some other pasta) for 6
Minced chives for garnish

Plunge the lobsters into a pot of boiling salted water and cook for 2 minutes. Remove and twist off the claws. Cool lobster bodies under cold running water. Meanwhile, return claws to the pot for 4 more minutes. Cool under running water. Extract all the meat from the lobster, reserving coral if either one is female, and refrigerate.

Heat the oil in a heavy pot. Sweat the onions, garlic, celery, carrot, and fennel until wilted—about 10 minutes. Add the thyme and tomatoes; simmer, uncovered, for 30 minutes. Add the paprika and simmer 5 minutes more. Season to taste with salt and pepper, and then stir in the cream.

Cook the pasta. Cut the lobster into bite-size chunks. When the pasta is 3 minutes shy of ready, add the lobster to the pot of sauce and stir to heat through. Fold in any coral. Drain pasta, reserving 1 cup of the cooking water. Toss the pasta with half the sauce and starchy cooking water to taste. Distribute among 6 warmed pasta bowls and top each with an extra ladle of sauce. Garnish and serve.

have never bought a pair of scales so it's no good asking me how much of anything"); the only precision he brings to the process is the insistence that you prepare the dish "to the accompaniment of a private bottle of Sancerre"—and then, when finished, open six (six!) more. Sean Connery provides a recipe for Spiced Beef with Parsley Dumplings, the great racing driver Stirling Moss does Veal Stroganoff, Roger Moore contributes his Potato Gnocchi, and Joan Collins adds a surprisingly fattening Pommes Paysanne. Then, in the "Puddings and Cakes" section, just after Tony Randall and Ronnie Barker, right before Nanette Newman, and Twiggy and Justin, you find the Mordecai Richler recipe for Noah's Apple Cake.

To the best of my knowledge this was his only published recipe. Even so, he wrote no introduction for it—which you can put down to modesty, if you like, or just to the fact that he had never watched carefully enough as my mother made it to have any insight into the process whatsoever (other than that he considered the finished product to be not just a great dessert but also—with a black coffee and cigar on the side—the healthy anchor of a complete breakfast). My mother's recipe was for a simple cake, heavy on sliced apple, subtly enlivened with shredded coconut and sultanas. Her cake was nonetheless quite light, for aside from the crumbly, sugared topping, it featured only enough dough to bind everything together and not a tablespoon more. She called it Noah's Apple Cake because she almost always made it for my older brother's birthday. I frequently requested it for mine too, and occasionally she conceded—which was nifty, as our respective celebrations fall just four days apart.

My mother's apple cake was conceived in her culinary heyday. But everyone must start somewhere. In my mother's case, it was not at home, where she mostly ate salad ("I can thank my mum for making me extremely healthy," she said to me, cryptically, of the lack of cooked meals in her youth). Moving on to war-ravaged London in 1947, where ration books were still in play, my mother made her initial foray into the role of dinner-party hostess in a one-room apartment near Marylebone Library, presenting a one-dish repertoire of scrambled eggs. Scrambled *goose* eggs, usually, as her butcher had passed along the hot tip that, because the egg coupon in her weekly ration book applied only to chicken eggs, she could by contrast purchase as many goose eggs as she could afford. In time, her first boyfriend passed along an even better tip to cook by—or more precisely, his father did. "Never cook with plonk," he told her. "Always use what you're drinking." What *he* was drinking was usually something from his family château in Bordeaux, and this cultural exposure helped my mother along some. Soon enough, she was making a decent boeuf bourguignon. This would mean nothing to her first husband ("Food was of little if any interest to him," she recalled of writer Stanley Mann. "If I gave him a boiled egg, he'd eat half."). But soon my father came along, and made it quickly clear that he was very much of the opposite persuasion. "Mordecai loved his meat and two veg, and I learned quickly that he was very appreciative of my efforts," she told me of their early days together. The novelist Ted Allan had introduced them; as it happened, his wife, Kate, was the first person my mother met who cooked both very well and seemingly effortlessly.

"I'll never cook that way," my mother recalls saying to Kate one day, after eating a lunch she had just prepared.

"It's easy," Kate replied. "Buy that book by Irma Rombauer."

I found that seminal edition of *The Joy of Cooking* on one of the upper shelves adjacent to the AGA. Published in the U.K. by J.M. Dent and Sons in 1952, it was printed with the lovely and long since abandoned subtitle *A Compilation of Reliable Recipes with an Occasional Culinary Chat.* Perhaps the subtitle was later dropped because so many of the "chats" were, too. Like, say, in the recipe for Chantilly Potatoes, which begins, "The following recipe is reminiscent of the old coloured man who said all he could find that college had done for his children was to put ma on 'lasses and pa on 'taters." The book was a treasure trove, the cover held together just barely with yellowed Scotch tape, with browning old scraps of paper protruding from its pages like the plates staggered along the back of a stegosaurus. The first crumbling newspaper clipping I extracted featured a recipe for spare ribs by the late Jehane Benoît, Canada's original celebrity chef, who recommended a special trip to an Asian market to procure the required pre-made hoisin and MSG. (Trust me, she was a lot more deft with French country cooking.) A recipe in the poultry section was bookmarked with an ancient shopping list, which began with two highly promising ingredients: "ducks, oranges." The next one I pulled out had my mother's handwritten recipe for her memorable cheese pie. Next the volume surrendered an old telephone message for someone to please call George Axelrod (the author of *The Seven Year Itch*, who died in 2003). At the back of the book an appendix extols the virtues of the newly invented electric blender ("it is so much better than its reputation, that of making an A1 alcoholic drink"). Tucked between that and the dangling back cover I found a typewritten sheet containing some ingenious instructions for determining the temperature of an oven in that trying era that preceded the invention of the non-contact infrared oven thermometer:

1—Heat oven

2—Place a piece of white kitchen paper in the oven for three minutes.

3—If paper is:

    Black—the oven is too hot

    Deep brown—the oven is very hot

    Golden brown—the oven is hot

    Light brown—the oven is moderately hot

    Light biscuit—the oven is slow

This struck me as indispensable wisdom for pinning to the cottage's kitchen wall. If instead you find it uselessly vague, be advised that subjective oven temperatures from "slow" to "very hot" were standard terms for cookbooks of the day. "Very hot" was defined as 450 to 500°F, "hot" meant 400 to 450°F, "moderately hot" was 300 to 350°F, and "slow" indicated a temperature of 250 to 300°F. Temperature ranges of fifty degrees were considered more than adequately specific. Cookbook writers had yet to embrace the pretense that cooking was a precise, paint-by-numbers activity, in which everything should always turn out tip-top regardless of a home cook's level of experience—as long as one followed the instructions. Recipes were a lot shorter then, too, and seldom lingered pedantically over process. You just had to try them, and learn.

And judging by the books on the shelves, my mother's learning curve had been steep. The more weathered volumes included *Traditional Recipes of the Provinces of France, Selected by Curnonsky* (*nom de plume* of Maurice Edmond Sailland, aka the Prince of Gastronomes, and co-author with Marcel Rouff of the twenty-eight-volume work *La France Gastronomique*). Curiosities like *The Alice B. Toklas Cookbook* shared shelf space with well-thumbed, stained, and once definitive tomes by Fernande Garvin, Robert Carrier, Simone Beck, and Elizabeth David. There was even a 1954 edition of *Tante Marie's French Kitchen*—an early translation of *La Véritable Cuisine de Famille par Tante Marie*, which to generations of French was a seminal cookbook, akin to *Mrs. Beeton's Book of Household Management*. Then there was a first edition (1968) of Jane Grigson's fantastic *The Art of Charcuterie*, which remains far more thorough than any trendily contemporary volume that I can think of. It also contains the following viscerally evocative scene from a small European village before the advent of refrigeration, when the annual slaughtering of pigs was of necessity and by design an autumnal ritual: "The pigs had fattened on acorns, Christmas was coming, the weather was cool and dry. The men sharpened their knives, and excited children soon ran—as they had done since Neolithic times and as they did in country villages until quite recently—to the terrible dying squeal of the pigs. It wasn't horrified sympathy that drew them, but the thought of bladder balloons."

What a waste; if those kids had only known that in 2012, at Epicure, in Hôtel Le Bristol in Paris, chef Éric Frechon would be peddling his take on the old Fernand Point classic of chicken baked in a pig's bladder—*poularde de Bresse en vessie*—for 260 a pop. My mother never tried that one. But my father did once relate to me with great delight the occasion of her presenting a whole roast suckling pig with an apple in its mouth to some gathered luncheon guests, some of whom promptly ran from the room, their hands clenched tightly over their mouths to prevent any accidents (a scene that he drew on, I always suspected, in *Solomon Gursky Was Here*, when Hyman Kaplansky scatters his gentile Seder guests by serving them matzo filled with fake baby's blood). Still, most of the food that we grew up with was less rarefied stuff. By the time that I was old enough to notice, she had largely settled into a groove of refined but robust European staples that kept my father sated and happy and not too, too fat: spaghetti Bolognese, osso buco Milanese, coq au vin, boeuf bourguignon, roast leg of lamb with flageolets, her excellent roast chicken, fish pie, and whatever other fish she could slip by *without mashed potatoes* that would not provoke too much complaint (wild Atlantic salmon and Dover sole were tolerated, but not much else). And that was how my mother got me started on the importance of cooking: with an education of the palate.

Next she imbued a sense of comfort about being in the kitchen. Because I was the youngest, when my older brothers and sisters were still at school or just didn't want me around, and my father was still at work, the kitchen was where I found her company. Of course, she gave me jobs to help make me feel useful. At age three or four, in England, I remember toddling off to the backyard of our house in Kingston upon Thames to fetch leaves from the bay laurel tree for her soups and stocks. By the time we moved to Montreal, I had graduated to far more complicated assignments, like sifting flour, a trick she had doubtlessly honed on my older siblings, guaranteed to keep me quiet in concentration for close to an hour. Next, in summertime, I picked up the concept of planning long term, when I was put on duty stirring macerated dried fruits for our Christmas cakes. But the actual need to cook anything more complicated than a fried egg, grilled steak, or broiled salmon steak did not arrive until I was a teenager, when suddenly my parents looked around, noted that all my siblings had left home, decided that they had enough with child-rearing, and upped stakes. They bought an apartment in Chelsea, London, a couple of blocks from Pierre Koffmann's La Tante Claire (now Restaurant Gordon Ramsay), and started wintering there, and summering in Memphremagog while abandoning me to fend for myself in a luxurious downtown Montreal apartment across the street from the Ritz-Carlton.

As a student with a part-time job, I quickly learned that the fine restaurants that my parents had so considerately introduced me to were very much out of my price bracket. Then I learned that cheap fast food was revolting no matter how much dope one smoked first (and I really tried). The same went for all that processed frozen food my mother had banned from the house to my considerable resentment when I was growing up. So whenever she was around, I tried to capitalize on it, pressing her hard for cooking lessons. I still have a folder of the recipes with which she got me started, and looking them over, I can easily recall my desperation for greater precision in her measurements and instructions.

"Mince some carrots—"

"How *many* carrots?"

"Oh, one or two."

Well, which is it for fuck's sake?

Other times, she was excessively specific. My old file rather incredibly contains a recipe with her instructions for Uncle Ben's Converted Rice. "Remember," it reads, "stock cubes may be salty so do not season until the very end." Fortunately I turned out to be a fast learner. Uncle Ben's quickly gave way to pommes Anna, and from her spaghetti Bolognese, I tried my hand at replicating on instinct the *poulet de grain—sauce moutarde* I liked so much at L'Express bistro on Rue Saint-Denis. And it was not nascent talent that drove this learning so much as an epiphanous, experience-based realization that girls dug boys who cooked. On that front too, my mother's tutelage was often useful. I remember, for example, early in university days, getting into a bit of a state one afternoon about what to cook for an imminent dinner for two, for it was a first date, the prey was almost absurdly fetching, and I so desperately wanted to get the meal right that I could not stop wavering on my menu. So I ran an idea by her.

"Oh *no*," she said, her tone heavy with disapproval. "I wouldn't make the duck à l'orange."

"But why?" I asked.

"Well, what will you do to impress her next?"

Good point. In my enthusiasm I had neglected to consider the possible requirement of a second date to close the deal, and in that tense eventuality, my repertoire had nowhere to go but down. And so it came to pass that I learned that when in doubt, it is always better to embrace and run with well-executed simplicity rather than risk overreaching one's grasp. (I still believe it now. But after nearly twenty years of writing about food, eating in great restaurants, hanging out in their chefs' kitchens, and collaborating with them on cookbooks, my idea of simplicity has evolved some.)

So what does an experienced home cook throw together for his mother, two brothers, two sisters, two children, and a niece over a weekend at the country when there is far too much to pack and no time to cook? There were some things I had no choice but to bring with me. Such as a side of smoked salmon from a chinook I had caught that summer in the Haida Gwaii. And bread, from Toronto's Petite Thuet, which, between chef Marc Thuet and his baker Martial Ribreau, turns out the best breads in the country. I do not just mean great baguette but *real* French bread: a sourdough *miche* as good as if not better than what you find at Poilâne, on rue du Cherche-Midi in Paris. I also had them toss in a few snacks to tide us over between proper meals: onion tarts, quiches lorraines, mountains of croissants, pains au chocolat, pain aux raisins to keep the children (young and old) happy. And I had ordered a couple of Thuet's dark farmer's rye, because for lunch one day I would be steaming up a smoked meat brisket sourced from Abie's—Montreal's finest—and it really does taste better on superior bread with real mustard. Other than that I would rely on local sourcing as much as possible. For dinners that meant leaning on the AGA and its proclivities for easy roasting, for the oven is all but guaranteed to reward your low effort with crisp, moist results. One night I would do some plump, organic chickens from Bio de Charlevoix and serve the birds with the easy accompaniment of roasted potatoes, carrots, and onions. For the next I would tap into the local duck supply and pop in a tray of Brome Lake Pekin duck confit, with a side of slender French green beans and wild rice, and a splash of port, red wine, and veal demi-glace reduction to dress things up a little. And that would pretty much do it—along with a fairly shocking amount of wine. My only regret is that I never did find that pie bird.

~ 2 ~

CHARCUTERIE

The fattest pig in the Toronto club district will invariably be found at Buca Osteria & Enoteca, near the intersection of King Street West and Portland Street. So when I dropped by one Monday early in May 2011, I was unsurprised to look in the walk-in fridge and behold the severed head and twin hanging sides of a genuine *suino pesante*—a voluptuous porcine stunner. The butcher had claimed that when she was still waddling she had tipped the scales impressively close to four hundred pounds. And four hundred pounds undressed was precisely what Buca executive chef Rob Gentile had been dreaming about. For when it comes to the art of charcuterie—of which Gentile is a master—that weight is the magic number. And especially so for prosciuttos, because four-hundred-pounders always have great legs, full buttocks, and good musculature. And if the pig got that way on a quality cereal diet, then good health and great flavour is all but guaranteed, too.

Gentile had known as much for some time. But it had been driven home with fresh resonance on a recent and long-awaited *salumi* fact-finding excursion to Italy, where he had spent a week as a *stage* in the hard-working company of the artisan farmer Carlo Pieri at his family estate, Azienda Agricola Poggio Stenti. The farm is in southern Tuscany, up in the hills that roll from the dormant volcano Monte Amiata all the way to Maremma. Carlo is the head of the third generation of Pieris to have worked that parcel of land. It includes an olive grove from which they press their own oil. And it comprises a vineyard, too, which yields much-lauded Tribolo and Pian di Staffa. But it was as usual the pigs that had piqued Gentile's interest: four-hundred-pound black pigs that Carlo Pieri raises largely on feed that he grows, mills, and mixes to his own highly particular formula.

"You expect pigs to eat slop and scraps out of a trough—at least that was the perception I had, and the image I remembered from when I was young," Gentile told me. "So it was kind of weird seeing them eat oats and grains and meal mixed up in a dry cereal. It's powdery and dry and they always had it stuck all over their faces when they finished eating, like they just put their heads in a chalk bin, which is pretty funny. They were the healthiest animals I've ever seen."

Five of those pigs were slaughtered each day at an abattoir two hours up the road, to which Pieri and Gentile drove the pigs themselves ("which was *interesting*," Gentile adds, "as the pigs were two and a half times my size"). *Il mattatoio* was impeccable ("like, in the middle of nowhere and it's spotless—*hospital*-clean—I was blown away"). While the pigs were being slaughtered, and the on-site inspectors undertook their meticulous examination of the organs to ensure that they were disease free, Gentile and Pieri passed the time sitting about with the other workers, snacking on *salsiccia cruda* (raw pork sausage) and various other *salumi* that Pieri had brought along from his aging cellar or from the family *bottega*, Macelleria Norcineria, in the village of Sant'Angelo Scalo, in Montalcino.

"He's a farmer who does it all—a real *norcino*," Gentile explained to me, deploying a term that Italians use to denote a *salumi* master, rather than someone who hails from the de facto *salumi* capital of Norcia, in Umbria. "It's the one trip I've been wanting to do ever since we opened."

This was in May 2011; Buca had opened in October 2009. The trouble with getting away any time sooner was that the restaurant had been a far greater success out of the starting gate than anyone involved in its planning had dared to hope. Part of that had to do with the fact that openings of quality restaurants like Buca were a rarity in recessionary 2009—in Toronto and just about everywhere. The element of surprise was that Gentile was just twenty-nine, had never been an executive chef before, and was not a known commodity around town outside of his industry. It was in fact the (Top) chef and restaurateur Mark McEwan who strongly suggested I pop down to club land and try Buca, for Gentile had worked for McEwan for seven years as a sous-chef at his restaurants Bymark, North 44, and One. In the process Gentile had undoubtedly learned something of the finesse, cost planning, and quality control that is the collective McEwan hallmark. And when Gentile applied all that to his true culinary passion—the food of his *nonna*—the results were golden. It took just one visit to persuade me that Buca was the best and most authentic Italian restaurant in town. Many others agreed, and there had been a waiting list for bookings most evenings since. Success was gratifying, but made it almost impossible for Gentile to get away. Until, in 2011, Buca's owners, Peter Tsebelis and Gus Giazitzidis, sensibly thought to make their young executive chef a partner. Various Buca spawn—starting with Bar Buca, nearby on King Street—were suddenly on the horizon, and the frequent travels to Italy that Tsebelis and Giazitzidis undertook to trawl pleasurably for fresh ideas to help move those projects along were now open to Gentile, too. The three generally travel together at first, and then Gentile splits off to do a *stage* somewhere, reconvening with Tsebelis and Giazitzidis in Rome. His first *stage* was at Poggio Stenti.

"'I thought I was pretty good, but I'm a novice," Gentile told me of how his *salumi* skills stacked up abroad, as he prepared to get to work on his new pig that sunny spring day. "There's so much refinement there compared to what we're doing here. This guy made pork liver sausage with gallbladder, cheek, and the bloody parts of the neck!"

Until then, said *mozzafegato* (which translates as "liver-killer," a moniker conceived in deference to its *fegato*-threatening richness) was not something one found hanging amongst the treasures in the glass-fronted Buca aging room. But on any given day there was plenty else of interest that could be seen dangling from the rafters—almost all of it prepared for the hook by chef Gentile. (His uncle had also contributed a cut or two.) Limbs were clearly a family specialty. Some had once belonged to lambs, others to wild boar, and even to goats. Once, I got a text message from Gentile suggesting I drop by to sample his newest take on Italian-Canadian *salumi*: prosciutto of bison leg. But most of the prosciuttos were pork: modest-sized legs, harvested from Yorkshire and Tamworth pigs, and other, massive ones plucked from their Rubenesque brethren, the Berkshire. There were liver-based *salumi*, and curing sausages made from minced horsemeat. Pancetta and other basics were always stacked high against the display window, which is across the corridor from the cellar in the passageway leading to the rear dining room. Most intriguingly— or at any rate, representing a first for me—a handful of items hanging there had *never* been ambulatory. Namely duck egg yolks, drying in pouches of cheesecloth until they became as firm as Parmigiano-Reggiano or a good pecorino and could be similarly grated over pizzas and carpaccios for an enriching kick. And today Gentile was planning on adding two new items to his ever-expanding catalogue: the aforementioned *mozzafegato* and a second freshly learned trick.

"Carlo taught me how to do prosciutto from the *shoulder*," Gentile related, his excitement palpable as he introduced this radical *salumi*-for-the-masses notion that each pig on earth might conceivably yield four prosciuttos rather than the conventional pair. "You have to bone it, to take the plate out—it's shaped sort of like a fish. And when you're done the cut looks fantastic. If you didn't know, you'd think it was a normal prosciutto from the hind leg."

Gentile wears his hair buzzed short, if not clean off, and he is fit and trim—rather shockingly so for a man so preoccupied with pork and its myriad fatty trimmings. But then, it takes a certain strength and agility to move whole sides of monster pigs around one's kitchen—especially a kitchen like that at Buca, which is long and narrow like a Roman slave galley. At the southern end you find the hot kitchen, with the grills, burners, and pizza ovens, wide open and overlooking the main dining room. But the prep kitchen, on the northern side, beyond the service bar, is fully enclosed. Which is a good thing, for this is where the butchery takes place.

Gentile and his (then) executive sous-chef, Ryan Campbell, began with the pig's right side, placing it gently on the counter lengthwise and skin side down. A row of plastic bins and bus pans had been arranged in a row along the back of the counter, some of them labelled for their contents, others speaking for themselves. The unlabelled tray bearing an inch-deep layer of coarse grey salt from Île de Ré clearly awaited individually filleted muscles of hind leg for prosciuttini, small fillets of prosciutto that cure far more quickly than a full leg. Hard back fat and firm, dark cuts of pork were destined for the bin labelled "salumi," and softer, paler meat and dry, crumbly fat would be placed in the tray labelled "finocchiona," to make the Tuscan pork sausage heavily seasoned with wild fennel seeds. Another, marked "mozzafegato," would take all the dark cuts from the neck and other tasty trimmings allotted to be mixed with pork liver and other offal for Gentile's inaugural run at this newly learned sausage. Some soft fat would be set aside for *sugnatora*, the mix of puréed fat, salt, and pepper that is smeared over raw legs of ham as insulation to keep them moist as they age and cure. Then there were large bins for the prized *cotenna* (skin) and bones, and finally, those off-*off*cuts destined for staff meals. Off to the side, filleting knives of varying lengths and rigidity were arranged in a row, along with the more rudimentary but equally necessary hacksaw.

"There's no way this pig was four hundred pounds. Why do they always do this to me? They call up and say, 'We've got one ready, we've got one ready.' *Sure* you do," Gentile muttered as he sized up his side of pork. And he continued grumbling as he assessed the location of the cut in the neck that severed the pig's head from the rest of the carcass. "The second vertebra is the second vertebra! I explained this to him ten times ... "

The head in question was standing upright on the stump of its neck at the end of the counter, eyes shut but with ears erect and seemingly alert. I could not help but think of the *Lord of the Flies*, glowering at Ralph and asking, "Aren't you afraid of me?"—but I did my best to instead stay focused on the crisis of the precise vertebral location of its decapitation. The crux of the issue is that if you cut higher than the second vertebra, you compromise the future *guanciale*, the cured jowl meat that must be used for making, say, a carbonara (even though the standard Americanized Italian recipe book typically suggests pancetta or, worse, bacon). If on the other hand you cut too low, you endanger the *coppa*—cured collar—or the prosciutto that could be cut from the shoulder.

As for the size of the animal, the fact of the matter is that while smaller pigs lend themselves beautifully to being cooked fresh, bigger ones are always better for the long-term, slow-maturing purposes of charcuterie. For the more developed musculature of a larger pig means more flavour, and the meat retains better texture when dry-cured, just as surely as the smaller animal will yield more supple, tender results after a stint on the grill or in the oven. Most pigs destined for cooking are slaughtered at an undressed weight no greater that 190 pounds. Keeping a few around until they reach double that weight throws the routine on the farm. Most farmers do not want Refrigerator Perry in the barnyard, disturbing the peace at the trough, so they get anxious to see large pigs dispatched to the slaughterhouse even as they crest three hundred pounds. Hence the possible exaggeration of this swine's weight over the phone.

Regardless, Gentile had already decided to proceed with a different supplier, one specializing in a different mix of heritage breeds. He did not like the way the Tamworth-Berkshire cross he had long been working with filled out when fattened beyond their conventional two-hundred-pound final weigh-in. "That bloodline is just no good for being slaughtered at four hundred pounds," Gentile explains. "At that weight their fat is just out of hand." So the chef had instead secured an exclusive-supply arrangement with Max and Vicki Lass at Church Hill farm in Punkeydoodles Corners, near Stratford, Ontario. They specialize in British heritage breeds like Jersey Red and Large Black, which when combined possess ideal qualities for a large pig: more intra-muscular fat, less flab, a good layer of top-quality back fat, and fine, crumbly, hard fat, too.

In the meantime Gentile had no choice but to proceed with what he had. To begin, he cut and pried free the ribcage in a single sheet that I was thinking would smoke nicely, for a magnificently Brobdingnagian rack of barbecued ribs. But Gentile had more

Italian plans: he would instead braise the ribs, and then shred the exceptionally tasty meat that lies between the bones for scattering over his *con cicorilli* pizzas. Moving on, the belly was trimmed and separated from the loin. The former would be shaped into a perfect rectangle and then cured as pancetta, while the latter, after a similar treatment, would become *lonzino*. The hind leg surrendered its muscles as individual fillets for the cause of prosciuttini, which would cure in months instead of the year or so required for a full prosciutto.

The second side of pork was cut very differently. Most of the hind leg was removed as a single large fillet, to be made into that most treasured of Italian hams, the *culatello*. First its fat was trimmed down to a reasonable covering, then it was tied into the customary pear shape, salted, and dispatched to cure in a cold room for a week. At that point of the *culatello* process in Italy, the ham would traditionally be wrapped in a pig's bladder, tied again, and hung up to cure in a cold, humid cellar teeming with eager mould spores. But here in Toronto, where pigs' bladders are all but impossible to procure, Gentile instead uses an envelope made from reconstituted natural sausage casings—intestines—which does close to the same job. After the ham is wrapped and tied again, the covering is punctured all over so that enzymes may properly penetrate the meat and do their tenderizing work. Then it would be strung up for many months.

As Gentile finished the *culatello*, Campbell was working on the rest of the fresh side. This time he kept loin and belly attached, trimmed it neatly, and seasoned it heavily with salt, garlic, and rosemary. Then he rolled the loin up snugly in its flap of belly, skin side out, and tied it in a roll. This, of course, is porchetta, the ultimate pork roast. "They did a nice job scalding the skin and getting the hair off it. It's really smooth. It's a nice pig to work with," Campbell said, making peace with the pig as he finished up with the prize cut. The massive roast was then whisked away to the oven, for even at high temperature it would take many hours to cook through and yield its inimitably crisp skin and moist, belly-insulated roast loin. The porchetta was scheduled as an evening special, and I was sorry that I would not be there to help eat it.

Gentile, meanwhile, was lost in the task at hand—butchering his first foreleg-and-shoulder prosciutto. He too had evidently come to terms with the pig, for rather than complain any more, he was stooped low over the cut he was working on, concentrating hard. He steered the tip of his filleting knife with the fingers of his left hand even as he grasped its handle in his right—to ensure superior accuracy in his cuts. Peeling back the skin and trimming a little of the fat from the shoulder appeared to be a fairly straightforward procedure. But extracting the blade bone from the shoulder was evidently no mean feat. Even with a filleting knife, it involved as much scraping as slicing. Cutting the muscle from the exposed inner side of the bone was the easy part. On the outside, though, there was virtually no insulating flesh between the bone and the skin that covered it, and the two were most stubbornly attached. If the skin was punctured while being separated from the bone, the cut of pork would no longer be usable as a prosciutto, because the boned shoulder needs the skin both for protection as it cures and for structural integrity as it hangs. "You break through, it's done," Gentile stated matter-of-factly. Finally, after nearly fifteen minutes spent crouched low over the troublesome bone, Gentile pried it free of the meat and skin around it, pivoted it upward from where it met the shoulder joint, and with a final stroke of his knife, triumphantly detached it.

"YEAH! I got it!" he barked as he stood up straight. "Not as good as Carlo—but good enough to cure!"

After a few more minutes of trimming and general prettification, the foreleg really did give a convincing impression of being a hind limb. Yes, it was a little slender in the shank. But the thick, perfect oval of pork perched on top of that, marbled and capped with generous layers of fat, lent the package convincing hind-leg heft. So the passing parade of sous-chefs and kitchen hands muttered in awe and admiration.

"That's a foreleg?!"

"Yes."

"No fucking way!"

The comments continued long after Gentile had wandered off—without saying a word, as if his new *trick* had been nothing. He then settled contentedly in the back dining room with a laptop, to write the evening menu. Campbell would take on the *salatura*—the salting—of the foreleg and the rest of the finishing up.

Buca means "pit," and the restaurant takes its name from its location, which is well below street level. A century ago it was the boiler room for the factory and warehouse buildings that still stand to either side of it. To get to Buca you must first enter a gated laneway off King Street and follow it to its end. Locate the discreet sign, open the glass doors alongside, and descend the curved staircase that overlooks the Buca lounge—which is not so much a draw in itself as a holding bay for diners awaiting tables in one of the two dining rooms that flank it. Once installed there and equipped with an aperitivo or a glass of wine, you may want to have a look around and marvel a little at how local enthusiasts of such hearty and authentic Italian food manage to stay so trim. But in time—if you are anything like me—your eyes will stray upward, over the bar, to the glass window on the aging fridge built into the wall above. A few large prosciuttos that will not fit in the main aging room are always hanging on display there, and the last time I checked, some nine months after I watched Gentile prepare his first shoulder prosciutto, the ham in question was hanging there amongst them, luscious and beckoning, but untouched. It was still not ready.

But fortunately the aging lockers at Buca are loaded with *salumi* that enjoyed a head start on that intriguing prosciutto. So if you order a *salumi* board there you will not miss it. In fact the Buca selection has never been better—in variety, or quality. When the restaurant opened, their cured ham usually came from Mario Pingue's Niagara Food Specialties. And while Pingue's prosciutto is occasionally excellent, to me it more often than not tastes like it was rushed through its aging paces to meet the burgeoning and generally forgiving local demand. Gentile's house-made prosciutto is a considerable improvement. And the better that prosciutto turns out, the more adventurous and experimental Gentile becomes.

Hence the bison leg. If he has some of that startlingly purple-hued meat on hand when you drop by, do try it, for its combination of assertive flavour and lean, dry bresaola-like texture combine for a unique experience. His *culatello* is supple and moist. Each of the cured sausages featuring liver or blood are rich and complex and not to be missed. Whether made of pork or lamb, his *coppa* is creamy and seductive. He also makes great lardo—cured strips of pure back fat—which he serves with an addictive fried bread common to Emilia-Romagna and Piedmont called *gnocco fritto*. These crisp, salty pillows of deep-fried dough puff up like pommes soufflées, and when you pierce them and then drape the lardo over the fresh, steam-billowing perforation, the cured fat is warmed and becomes even softer and creamier for it.

All the same, I have to say that almost all of the women I have taken to Buca have proved immune to its charms. Neither do they much warm to the idea of Gentile's *salsiccia cruda*, the raw pork sausage Chef serves exclusively on days when he butchers a fresh pig. The *salumi* and charcuterie phenomenon has generally not been a treasured development for the female diner, who, under perennial pressure to stay trim, generally knows that you do not get or stay that way when you snack regularly on strips of unadulterated fat. Many men feel the same way. One of the most intriguing things about the trend of the charcuterie board is that—rather like the tasting menus that ruled fine dining five years previous—it is often more of a chef's playground and showcase than it is about pleasing the majority of the customers. Innumerable chefs have told me over the years that they do not sell charcuterie in a manner even close to reflecting the coverage the items receive in the food pages. Even at the peak of the trend, in 2008, chef Mark McEwan, who probably knows numbers as well as or better than anyone else in the industry, told me that no other dish on any of his menus would keep its place there if it sold as little as did the charcuterie board at Bymark. Bymark's was a good one, too, with two excellent terrines (one foie gras, the other rabbit and squab) that were prime examples of the sort of thing one should sensibly order in restaurants—because they take many tedious hours to make, and there was no way of preparing a batch that was not twenty times larger than what a home cook needed or wanted. All the same, few ordered it—but food writers wrote about it.

When I was the food writer and restaurant critic at the *National Post*, in the early 2000s, I was doubtless one of those charcuterie proponents who did not stop to consider the true level of public appetite for fatty, salty cured meats. But with good reason: my justification was entirely selfish. For one of the more difficult aspects of moving to Toronto from Montreal, as I did in 1995, was the local dearth of decent pâtés, terrines, and cured sausages. Procuring a pricey terrine of foie gras was never a problem. But the day-to-day necessities that I had long been accustomed to keeping in the fridge for a ready snack even on a university student's budget—pâté de campagne, say, or terrine of rabbit with pistachios, or *mousse de foies de volailles*—were suddenly all but impossible to come by. When you did manage to find them they were priced like delicacies instead of staples, and even then, the quality was dodgy. You did not go to the store and pick what you wanted freshly sliced from a selection of terrines a dozen strong, as at any Quebec supermarket. Instead you picked from squashed, aging vacuum-packaged pre-sliced cuts of greying terrines that invariably tasted of bread crumbs and other mealy filler. The only rillettes to be found in town were imported from New York State, where they were manufactured at the D'Artagnan factory, which churned the stuff out as chunky as steak and kidney pie. On the cured-sausage front, no one seemed to have heard of *gendarmes* or *rosettes de Lyons.* And needless to say, in a town where chefs made the front of the food section just for grilling a bit of horsemeat that you can find at any Métro supermarket in Quebec, chances of finding a nice dried horsemeat-spiked sausage like *saucissons d'Arles* were nil.

So when local chefs made their initial moves into the arena of charcuterie, it seemed essential to hungrily applaud whenever possible. When the Oliver-Bonacini restaurant group opened an upscale bistro in downtown Toronto called Biff's with rabbit rillettes on the menu, I overlooked the fact that there was butter in the mix instead of animal fat sourced from a rabbit or pig and just praised it for being smooth and for containing meat that had been properly shredded. And a few years later, when rather basic terrines and pâtés started showing up incongruously on expensive tasting menus—say, a veal-cheek-in-aspic number served to me as a course in a $150 menu at the now defunct Perigee, in Toronto's Distillery District—I did my best to eat my fix and keep the giggling private.

Soon, those early murmurings of discovery in charcuterie began to snowball. In 2006, cured Serrano ham from Spain arrived noisily in town and immediately began appearing with much fanfare on our most expensive menus—even francophile ones, like The Fifth's, the once great French restaurant tucked over a club on Richmond Street. Local food writers fell over themselves to praise the stuff; one restaurant critic (okay, it was Amy Pataki at the *Toronto Star*) even described, in a review of Chris McDonald's Cava, how the taste of the fat of the Serrano hinted "at the acorns the pigs had grazed on." Alas, she must have looked up the wrong ham in the dictionary, for the famous *jamón ibérico*, or *pata negra*, which does graze on acorns, were still not being legally imported here. Neither were any decent Serrano hams, because Spain was still assessed as a risk for "classic swine fever," and the only Serrano ham that was being legally imported was the cheap, mass-market stuff that the Spaniards make with pigs sourced from countries free of swine fever such as Holland, Sweden, and Denmark. If you wanted to taste acorns in your cured ham, you would have to wait another two years for the import of *pata negra* to Canada to become legal.

Or—if like me you lacked that kind of patience—you could instead slip $300 in cash to a certain restaurateur in Little Portugal who each Christmas thoughtfully smuggled a dozen-odd full bone-in legs of *pata negra* vacuum-packed and buried in containers of Mediterranean fish. Or you could lean on a Toronto distributor of fine Quebec cheeses—Cole Snell, founder of Provincial Fine Foods—who by late 2006 had secured an exclusive deal for importing fabulous prosciuttini from an Iowa farmer and *charcutier* named Herb Eckhouse, whose company, La Quercia, made a ham labelled *rossa* from Berkshire pigs that grazed on acorns. These were heady days for lovers of pork cookery, which is all that *charcuterie* really means.

And thinking back to those glorious times, I have to hand it to chef Marc Thuet for presenting charcuterie in the form that I consider to be its apotheosis (even if the chef disagrees). Choucroute garnie first appeared on the menu at his restaurant Bistro and Bakery Thuet, on King Street West, in the dark days of winter, 2005, brightening it immeasurably on the spot. I had first eaten choucroute garnie in 1990 in Paris, with my mother and my father, who was on a book tour for the French publication of *Solomon Gursky Was Here*. After landing at Charles de Gaulle airport we proceeded directly to Saint-Germain-des-Prés, stopping at Hotel Duc de Saint Simon only long enough to drop our bags and then reconvene in the lobby. From there we headed six blocks (by taxi—my father was hungry) to Brasserie Lipp, one of his old hangouts from the fifties.

It was my first meal in Paris and so I can still recall settling in there and eagerly sizing up the menu—and my slight confusion at learning that this exercise was academic, for my father had long before decided that we were going to share a large platter of choucroute garnie. That was what *he* wanted. But as it happened I had long imagined my first lunch in Paris being something more like sole amandine or tournedos Rossini or *canard à la presse*, so I protested a little at the prospect of instead tucking into a boring heap of sausages and sauerkraut. And then my mother confused me no end by declaring that she was opting to partake of the platter, too. This was very odd, because she almost always perceived being in a restaurant as one of those rare, privileged occasions when she could enjoy a quality piece of fish, without my father complaining about having to eat it too.

"Trust me," she said, with a conspiratorial nod.

So choucroute it was, all around. And what an education it proved to be: the mildly tangy sauerkraut, fragrant with juniper, studded all over with wonderfully tender iterations of pork, from tender, poached shank of ham, barely held together by its skin, to the *saucisses de Strasbourg* that burst juicily forth from their casings with an audible pop as they surrendered to your hungrily advancing teeth. I thought it was divine.

"I can't believe how many people tell me that choucroute is the first thing they ate in Paris," Thuet said to me disparagingly when I told him the story. "I just think, 'You went all the way to Paris for a fucking *choucroute*?' Seriously?"

Thuet hails from Blodelsheim, in Alsace, which is choucroute central, though you will find versions of the dish in neighbouring Lorraine and in parts of Germany. Choucroute did not in fact grow popular in Paris until the end of the Franco-Prussian War, when Alsace and Lorraine were annexed as part of the new German empire and Alsatian refugees made a break for the City of Light— at that time, the Paris Commune. Some of them, such as Leonard Lipp, opened restaurants specializing in their native cuisine (and beer). So Brasserie Lipp opened, like many other Parisian brasseries, in 1871, the second (and final) year of the war, and has been a draw ever since for Parisians and tourists alike. Mostly the latter, of late. Thuet was right: Paris is a long and expensive way to go for sauerkraut with all the trimmings. Especially when there weren't that many trimmings. For the Lipp version turns out to be authentic but spare. It is quite like the nearly century-old recipe from La Maison Kemmerzell, in Strasbourg, included in my

Traditional Recipes of the Provinces of France, Selected by Curnonsky, which features only smoked pork belly, pork loin, and *saucisses de Colmar*. Such minimalism is sometimes a source of pride. As the celebrated Alsatian artist and French war hero Jean-Jacques Waltz—better known as Oncle Hansi—explained of the recipe, "This is not … the sort of over-complicated, over-elaborate recipe, over-loaded with strange ingredients, that certain scatterbrained fervents of freakish gastronomy would like to impose upon us. It is truly a home-style recipe, the real recipe for good sauerkraut, as our good Colmar housekeepers prepare it."

Evidently they live larger in Blodelsheim than in Colmar. Or at any rate, *garnie* means something extra to the Thuet family. For his recipe only begins like the others—with sauerkraut made from the large-headed, pale green cabbage named Quintal d'Alsace. Our green cabbage is close enough. But slicing it, packing it with salt and juniper berries, and pressing it until it ferments is not something you want to do at home in the city or on the site of a nice restaurant.

"It stinks," Thuet explained to me then. "Back home we stopped making it when my grandmother died. That was in 1995. The basement still fucking stinks. When you ferment the cabbage, the mould gets in the walls and never goes away."

In other words it is best to buy your sauerkraut from someone else (but avoid the Polish variety, which is sugared and does not work with the dish). Next you need *saucisses de Strasbourg*, which, when in Montreal, I used to buy for Thuet at Pâtisserie Belge on Avenue du Parc (the veal wieners at some Polish delicatessens make an acceptable facsimile). Then for the full Thuet treatment you also need *boudins blancs, boudins noirs, saucisses de Montbéliard,* smoked pork loin, ham hocks, and smoked speck— for when Thuet thinks *garnie,* he means it.

"I think it's the only dish in the world that has so many meats," Thuet allowed of his highly elaborate choucroute— which, had it been invented in Toronto, could have been called Pork Seven Ways. "It's nearly too much. But in Alsace we think it's not enough, so as well as the cabbage you have to serve potatoes."

You can bake potatoes for the purpose, boil them in their skins, or even deep-fry them. Thuet always served trimmed pommes vapeurs. Because that was what his mother did. "In France you always cook choucroute like your mum cooks it. What I learned from my mum is that if you put it all in the pot together you get greasy sauerkraut. You have no fat control. So what you do," Thuet elaborated, "is sweat the onions in a bit of goose or duck fat, fold it into the choucroute, cook it with some Alsatian Riesling or Cristal d'Alsace, poach the ham and sausages, fry the *boudins,* and put it all together at the very end. My mother makes a mean choucroute."

So did Thuet, especially in the later years before the restaurant closed (in 2010), when he made all the constituent sausages in-house. My favourite of them is the *boudin noir,* the classic sausage of pigs' blood that Thuet still occasionally sells through his Toronto chain of *traiteurs,* Petite Thuet. The only *boudin* in Toronto that rivals it is the one made by chef David Lee, co-owner of Nota Bene restaurant. The primary difference between them is that Lee dices the pork back fat that's stirred into the blood into a slightly smaller brunoise, which does not so much make the sausage less rich as less utterly overwhelming. Lee adds more chestnut flour, too. His is a truly great *boudin*—and he is typically open about how the recipe came to him.

In Lee's native London, the *boudin* is easy to come by, from the corner butcher to the Food Hall at Harrods. Served with nothing more than a side of mashed potatoes and sautéed apple, the *boudin noir* is a cheap and satisfying bistro staple. Just as it is in Montreal, where one evening in 2007, Lee popped in to Au Pied de Cochon, that highly entertaining but rather unjustly celebrated ode to the pig on Avenue Duluth, in the Plateau. He ordered the *boudins*. And thankfully it was an unusually good night for the kitchen there, and the *boudins* were not grainy from having been frozen or made with frozen blood (as when I tried them) but were instead the best blood sausages that Lee had ever tasted. So he summoned the chef, Martin Picard, told him so, and in exchange came home with the recipe. The ingredient that had pleased him so much was chestnut flour—a tweak Picard had presumably borrowed from the French *boudin* of Auvergne. And when Lee got back to his restaurant kitchen (then at Splendido, on Harbord Street), he started to play around with the Picard formula to make it his own.

The first time I sampled it after he got it right was at the bar at Splendido—a mere sliver, plated alongside some offal from the very opposite end of the price spectrum: seared foie gras (a good pairing, which I had enjoyed previously). After a few variations on that theme came Lee's porcine pièce de résistance: a six-inch disc of crisp and buttery puff pastry topped with duxelles, Taleggio cheese, arugula, pulled suckling pig, crisp crackling, sliced *boudin*, bacon, and pork jus. He launched the dish on the opening night of Nota Bene, on Queen Street West, before the restaurant even had a liquor licence (which is why to this day the *boudin* tart always makes me think of drinking Nebbiolo out of a coffee cup). And it stayed on the menu for a full year before retreating to the back catalogue and being relegated to occasional appearances as a daily special.

For me that *boudin* and suckling tart is the ultimate lofty expression of pork in Hogtown. The odd thing about the rise of the pig and all its constituent charcuterie there over the last decade is that it has occurred under the broad umbrella of what most people consider to be haute cuisine. Every high-end restaurant in town has had a run at some sort of charcuterie board or at least a variation on braised pork belly plated with seafood (lobster, scallop, crab, or black cod). Roast suckling pig specials have proliferated, and with them, elaborate farming backstories about heritage breeds like Berkshire and Red Wattles, or ordinary Yorkshires fattened on cream or whey. I enjoy all that, but wish it would show up more at the corner bistro, too. Pig is supposed to be pedestrian, not fine dining. In agrarian England the pig is known as "the gentleman who pays the rent," not the one who makes car payments on the Porsche. So I am impatient for the newly acquired rarefied pork sense to trickle down to affordable, old-fashioned simplicity and the corner bistro (or pub). For as great as that *boudin* tart may be, there are days when I do not want my blood sausage dressed up with puff pastry and arugula, but rather crave two plump ones

Suckling Pig and Boudin Tart

Chef David Lee

Serves 6

2 sheets top-quality puff pastry
1 egg, lightly beaten
3 *boudins noirs*
6 strips top-quality maple-glazed bacon
1/2 warm roast suckling pig with crackling
Salt and pepper
Oil for deep-frying
1 cup (250 mL) duxelles
1 cup (250 mL) grated Taleggio cheese
3 cups (750 mL) lightly packed washed young spicy arugula
1/2 cup (125 mL) pork jus, at a simmer

Preheat oven and deep-fryer to 375°F (190°C).

On a floured work surface, roll the puff pastry to a thickness of about 1/8 inch (3 mm). Then cut it into six 6-inch (15 cm) discs and transfer to a baking sheet lined with lightly buttered parchment paper. Brush pastry with beaten egg and bake until puffed and golden—10 to 15 minutes. Leave baked discs on the baking sheet. Meanwhile, fry the sausages until browned all over and heated through. Set aside. Fry the bacon until crisp; drain on paper towels. Pull meat from the suckling pig in 1-inch (2 cm) chunks, cover, and set aside in a warm place. Cut crackling into bite-size morsels and deep-fry until crisp. Drain on paper towels and season generously with salt and pepper.

Spread 2 tbsp (30 mL) of duxelles on each disc of puff pastry. Scatter cheese overtop, distributing it equally among the 6 discs of pastry. Follow with a handful of arugula. Top with about 4 chunks of warm suckling pig. Slice *boudins* into 1-inch (2 cm) lengths and distribute them equally among the tarts, standing the segments upright on their ends. Follow with a few shards of crackling. Return tray of tarts to the oven for 3 or 4 minutes. Transfer tarts to warmed plates, drizzle with pork jus, and serve.

in a starring role on the plate, with nothing for company but potato purée, sautéed apples, and a dollop of quality mustard. Thankfully Lee understands: sometimes, if I ask nicely, he lets me take some *boudins* home.

3

FISH

The chosen bait with which to troll for salmon in the frigid waters of the northern Haida Gwaii is the indigenous herring. And so at a fishing camp like The Clubhouse, the premier Langara Island outpost of the West Coast Fishing Club, each morning when you pack up your boat at the docks for a run to the fishing grounds, you are allotted a cooler full of the oily fish. And these herring are not alive but very much dead, the ice in their veins laced with mysterious preservatives that help keep them looking fresh, firm, and perky even as they endure the posthumous indignity of being dragged about under water at speed with a pair of hooks shoved through them.

Chef David Hawksworth, of the eponymous Hawksworth Restaurant at the Rosewood Hotel Georgia, in Vancouver, showed me the routine on my first day out on the water. To begin, you plunge your already chilly hand into the cooler of fish-blood-tinged slush and extract one ice-cold, slippery herring. Next, using a sharp knife, you decapitate it—but on an angle sufficiently sharp as to induce spin as the little fish is pulled through the water. Use the point of your knife to extract its frozen guts, and then mount the modified fish onto a pair of hooks. At this point a personal flourish may enter into the equation. Some anglers have a way of threading the length of leader between the hooks inside the belly of the herring rather than wrapping it around the outside, with a view to added stealth. Others cut a fresh wedge into the fish where its anus used to be, to improve water flow through the belly cavity. One Haida dockworker had a unique and absurdly complicated technique that after much fanfare appeared to make his herring spin twice as fast as anyone else's—but what with the preference of the salmon being unknown, none of us even bothered to attempt to replicate it.

"We give these salmon too much credit anyway," announced one of my fishing partners, Mark Davidson, a long-time Vancouver sommelier who now works for Wine Australia, shrugging off the demonstration as we pulled away in the boat. "All this fussing about how your herring spins is ridiculous. When they're in a biting mood, they'll take anything you put in front of them."

I was with him on this. And our basic approach proved perfectly acceptable to the big fish whenever they were in a suicidal mood. Better yet, it kept the manhandling routine with the slimy, cold herring down to a minimum. This was important not just for the obvious reasons but because of a story I had been told on my first day at camp. The tale was doubtlessly exaggerated in the telling, but no matter. Apparently, a few years previous, some unilingual Japanese had come to stay there, and whether as a product of rampant bravado—or just chauvinism trumping their lack of experience—they had declined a local fishing guide so that they could instead fish the tricky waters all by themselves. So off they went into the unknown, and after a time, they got peckish.

Alas, as they spoke no English they had missed a few important points in their pre-fishing briefing. For example, they did not know that even in the most insalubrious conditions, the highly civilized West Coast Fishing Club regularly dispatches crew in a Zodiac to hunt down chilly fishermen and offer them sustenance. Seriously: out there amidst the driving rain and the churning surf, they pull up alongside your fishing boat and lob various packages and snacks your way, all of them plucked directly from the Zodiac's electrically warmed storage bins. Say, a hot croissant packed full of scrambled eggs and bacon, a Thermos of hot coffee or tea, you name it.

Not knowing that, and lost and hungry, and clueless as to what to do with their fishing rods, the Japanese had taken matters into their own hands. So when the Zodiac driver approached their boat, the first thing he noticed was that none of them were fishing. And then as he pulled up alongside, worried, he saw that all the Japanese were seated cross-legged on the floor, gathered in a tight circle around their bait cooler, having a nibble. Now every time I selected a slimy herring from our cooler, I pictured those unfortunate Japanese tucking in for a snack, and could not stop myself from trying to imagine their conversation.

"Does anyone have any wasabi? This B.C. sushi is awful."

"It really stinks!"

"Shut up and eat. You must keep up your strength so that we can get out of here."

Thinking about it made me giggle, but it also made me feel mildly seasick. I persevered, and having baited another set of hooks, I clipped the line to the downrigger (a softball-sized metal ball that drags the bait down low, to where the salmon lurk and feed), let it go, clamped the rod into the trolling bracket, set the drag, and kicked back to watch tip and line. You might think that when a muscular chinook salmon has decided to make your herring its next snack, the good news would be telegraphed up from the depths loud and clear—that your rod would take a sudden and violent bow. But when trolling it cannot, for it is already bent back on itself nearly double from the drag of your trailing tackle and downrigger. The strike of a good fish can get easily lost in the mix. You must watch for signs very closely.

In fact you need to watch with all the vigilance of those circling eagles and hawks that now and then swoop low to take away discarded bait—or a tired salmon, just released and too exhausted and stunned to dive to safety. You need to focus without letting your eyes stray to the rugged beauty of the coastline, to the pillars of rock that rise from the water so dramatically, with their odd caps of moss and clinging, scraggly trees. Because if you look away too long you'll never know if you just missed your bait being discreetly stripped from your line by a cunning coho, leaving you trolling a useless, empty pair of hooks. If that were so, it would be time to reel in and reload. But what if you guessed wrong, your bait was still there, and at that very moment the largest, fiercest tyee to ever work the coast was sizing it up, gnashing his cruel, hard piscine lips and all set to pounce—only to back off, confused, because you reeled in too soon?

Some are a lot better at this fishing game than others. When I first visited Langara, in July 2011, I was a novice at trolling for Pacific salmon—although a couple of decades earlier, on the opposite coast, I used to go fly-fishing with my father for their Atlantic brethren, and between us we reeled in quite a few. Hawksworth, meanwhile, was an old hand. He had been fishing at the West Coast Fishing Club for a decade. And he was enjoying his seventh consecutive season there as the featured guest chef for their annual culinary retreat, a one-of-a-kind fishing trip wherein each evening features a gastronomic tasting menu helped along by a bottle-toting sommelier (usually the aforementioned Mark Davidson). Hawksworth certainly knew the ropes, and all that practice had obviously helped. As the affable, long-time Clubhouse manager Terry Cowan confided to me over a malt whisky late one night, Hawksworth had been a lousy fishermen when he first came to them. But somewhere along the learning journey he had acquired a new fishing-camp nickname: Killer.

It did not take long out on the water with Hawksworth to clock that his fishing reflexes were quick and his focus intense. One tap on a rod and he was on it as if putting out a grease fire in his restaurant kitchen in the middle of a dinner rush. In a flash he would have the rod out of its bracket, yank it hard to rip the line from its clamp on the downrigger down below, reel in fast to take back the fresh slack in the line, whip the rod back hard to set the hook in the fish, and resume reeling as furiously as he could. The fish tend to submit to this at first, but when they catch a first glimpse of the boat, their mood changes, and they turn around fast, flashing a long, broad silvery flank in the sunlight before running off again the other way against the drag. Play them right and they will tire and submit to the net. Play it wrong and they will shake the unbarbed hook from their mouth and return unharmed to the depths. Hawksworth won far more of these battles than he lost, and invariably, it was not long before another fish was in the boat, pinned down by netting as Hawksworth clobbered him on the head with a steel pipe.

Killer Hawksworth is in his forties now, but despite a working life spent sleeping too little and working excessive hours in the pallor-inducing setting of fluorescent-lit kitchens, he maintains boyish looks and could easily pass for younger. Some find him shy, even aloof; I would instead describe him as reticent. All the same, when out on the water, consumed by the relaxing distraction of good fishing, wry asides escaped him unchecked. Speaking of life at home with his four-year-old son, he said to me: "It's like having a member of al Qaeda living in your house—you have to be on guard all the time. Anything can happen. He has no remorse." One day we watched an angler on a boat nearby release a chinook that must have weighed over sixty pounds. As it disappeared back into the depths, Hawksworth said, "Now he's telling his friends, 'You wouldn't believe what just happened to me … I was abducted by aliens …'"

Another time he inadvertently revealed that once you have been trained to look at things from the perspective of a chef, it never quite goes away. "Do you know how much food that is?" he complained to me as we watched another angler pose for pictures with a forty-five-pounder he had elected to kill rather than to release. "They'll never eat that. That's one hundred meals." As we fished on, I worked through the math. From forty-five pounds, take away head, fins, and guts, get twenty-five pounds of salmon fillets. At a restaurant-standard five to six ounces per serving, I arrived at about eighty portions. Close enough.

One day the fishing was uncharacteristically slow and I got skunked—the only salmon I hooked got scoffed by a sea lion before I could reel him home. Come late afternoon, Hawksworth was in the Clubhouse kitchen working on the evening's five-course dinner when word came down that a guide on a boat being tossed about on the distant stormy waters off the northern tip of the island had just radioed in that he had picked up numerous sonar images of large bait balls in the waters between the reefs that straddle the Langara lighthouse. Clusters of bait—like herring—always attract larger fish to feed on them, and the word was that the salmon were there, and biting enthusiastically. Dinner for forty was still a couple of hours off. And what are sous-chefs for, anyway? Hawksworth laid down his chef's knife, I downed my whisky, and we made a dash for it.

We arrived at the lighthouse half an hour later in waters so rough that we could not stand up in the boat without holding on to something. Two other boats from our camp were fishing alongside us, but the waves were surging so high that we could seldom see them until they were all but on top of us. Then Hawksworth would fire the throttle and move off, with our lines trailing us in the chaos. After fifteen minutes we had two small chinook in the boat and called it a day. The ride back to camp was insane. We were airborne a good part of the time, as if riding on a Sea-Doo rather than in a nineteen-foot Boston Whaler. The outboards screamed as they churned air instead of water, and the ride was far too rough to enable sitting down. We rode standing—just—to better absorb the shocks of the ride, and clutched the poles to either side of the windscreen for balance.

"Has a chef ever put you in this much danger?" Hawksworth yelled over the din as we crashed from wave to wave through the surging, freezing spray.

"Sure!" I yelled back. *"Fugu!"*

He looked impressed. So impressed that I had to come clean and admit that I had never in fact eaten poisonous puffer fish, and was having him on. Back on shore, Hawksworth finished putting his meal together in a frenzy. It had a theme, and he called it "Bistro Classics." But it was clearly a very English bistro that he had in mind, and it had one foot in the past, the other in the present. We would begin with a truffled velouté of English peas, and follow with chinook tartare, a summer vegetable salad with Salt Spring Island goat's cheese, and finally a beef Wellington with puréed shallot red wine jus. Even his Italian dessert—vanilla panna cotta—got an English lift with some champagne-poached strawberries.

Hawksworth's guest-chef gig also involved cooking demonstrations. He did two while I was there, and unsurprisingly both involved fish, and both handily demonstrated his new, more accessible and casual approach to cooking. The finesse with which he made his name in Canada, at the Vancouver restaurant West, was still much in evidence, and so too the highly developed sense of colours on the plate. But the compositions were less subtle and more playful. For his first dish he lightly poached skinless fillets of chinook salmon belly in olive oil, then placed them over a South Asian–flavoured cucumber salad, against the stark black backdrop of a smear of squid-ink-dyed purée of eggplant. The second was a Japanese-Mexican-Italian concoction lifted from the opening menu at Hawksworth Restaurant: a carpaccio of tuna dressed with yuzu and soy and draped over lime-spiked avocado purée, sprinkled with batonettes of jicama and cucumber for crunch.

"Maybe I should try that with salmon instead?" Hawksworth said to me, when he was done.

It would work, of course. But to my taste dishes conceived with tuna in mind never taste as good when executed with salmon. The proposed change was as much about taste and texture as it was about sustainable, local sourcing. If you consult the Ocean Wise website, where marine biologists from the Vancouver Aquarium rate fish on their appropriateness for the plate based on the health of their stocks, the methods by which they are fished, and so on, you will find that chinook from northern B.C. get an unqualified recommendation for consumption, while yellowfin tuna comes with caveats. They are generally fine to eat if they are caught by pole fishing or trolling—unless they come from the Indian Ocean. And one is also supposed to avoid those harvested by long line or purse seine nets. Alas, all yellowfin look pretty much the same on ice.

The name of the centuries-old Spanish dish of *escabèche*—inspiration for the Belgian *escavèche*, the Italian *escabecio*, and the North

African *scabetche*, among others—is thought to be derived from the Spanish word *cabeza*, which means "head." So it is not surprising that the culinary process behind it begins with summary decapitation—just like preparing herring for trolling bait. Then you fillet the fish, lightly sear them, and marinate them for a day or so in a fragrant and mildly spicy brew rich in aromatics and heavily spiked with vinegar. If you were a sensible chef with one foot planted solidly in the Old World and an eye keenly fixed on the trends of the New, you might well one day turn your mind to applying this ancient technique to one of its most typical victims, the common sardine, but in the process, seek to give it a modern twist. And that was exactly what was sitting on a plate in front of me, as prepared by executive chef Frank Pabst of the Blue Water Café in Vancouver: a pair of sardine fillets, properly browned but barely cooked through, tangy with marinade, warm to the touch, and draped prettily—as prettily as a headless sardine can manage—over a bed of lightly pickled onion, with a little purée of sweet apple to one side and crème fraîche laced with caviar dabbed all around.

Chef's thinking struck me as just right. For his light touch—undercooked sardine, mild marinade—amounted to an acknowledgment that a dish conceived as a method of preservation in those terrible days before the refrigerator, or even the icebox, still features flavours that work well together, as long as you turn their intensity down a level, from cover-up to enhancement. Second, adding a lofty ingredient like caviar to pretty much anything is generally a good idea. And doing so with a pedestrian peasant dish like *escabèche* was very much attuned to the culinary thinking of the times (think Daniel Boulud's truffle-and-foie-gras-enhanced hamburger or, closer to home, Martin Picard's foie-gras-topped poutine). The dish was further helped by the fact that it was early November, and so prime season for sardines. (Eat them raw at a Japanese restaurant in the fall and you cannot fail to notice the thick layer of fat that their summer diet piles on beneath the skin for the long winter ahead, just as we would do, if we were not beset with the fear and hope that potential sex partners were watching.) The mild pickling in a red vinegar marinade handily offset that oiliness, the lightly pickled onion cozies up with it just as comfortably as happens in a jar of herring, and the caviar elevated the sum of the parts from bistro cooking to unpretentious fine dining.

The *escabèche* in question was the opening salvo in a menu conceived to celebrate a selection of abundant but admittedly unglamorous fish-next-door that Pabst, in a culinary nod to seafood sustainability and the environment at large, terms his "unsung heroes." Item number two was pan-seared mackerel, served crispy-skin side up on a bed of beet brunoise, dressed up with elderberry sauce and shavings of a surprisingly potent early-winter truffle. Next came mild-cured herring—skinned, cross-hatched on the grill, and placed atop sliced fingerling potatoes and onions, with a warm cream sauce laced with a little more caviar. Then there was white sturgeon, pan-roasted and then balanced on two shoots of salsify, with a smudge of cauliflower purée, sautéed chanterelles, stewed lentils, and a sprinkling of julienned red cabbage. The fish was succulent and meaty, and a good reminder that even fish-farm by-product can be a lovely thing. (It is caviar that justifies the sturgeon farm; the fish that create it are little more than a necessary inconvenience.) Last came sablefish, its marinade of sake and brown sugar bronzed from the grill, with an enticingly buttery potato purée to one side and an array of slender French green beans to the other, with a drizzle of rich veal jus all around.

Pabst likes robust flavours. His cooking strikes big, deep notes. These dishes all reference a youth spent immersed in the flavours of Germany and Belgium. His sardines with crème fraîche, lightly seasoned with coriander seed, make me think of the flavour profile of that classic German street food, herring on a bun. And his semi-cured grilled mackerel on fingerling potatoes brought to mind that classic French bistro dish *salade hareng-pommes à l'huile*. I put this to the chef when he came over to say hello and goodnight as I was on my way out the door.

"I can't help it," Pabst said, with a smile and a shrug. "That's the only way my fingers know how to dance!"

It was a good line but not quite true. For it was also evident that he enjoys playing out a bit of class war on the plate (pedestrian sardines and herring both plated with caviar, mackerel with truffles, and so on). On other nights he has prepared dishes that were purely Asian in nature (say, jellyfish seasoned with toasted sesame seeds, sesame oil, soy sauce, chili flakes, pink peppercorns, and julienned green onion). Another time he applied the Spanish accent of chopped chorizo to some sautéed flying squid, and then made a culinary excursion to Tunisia to fetch some harissa for some local Humboldt squid. Pabst's fingers may be in their comfort zone in central Europe, but they are convincingly multilingual.

The Blue Water Café anchors a five-block strip of restaurants, bars, and cafés clustered along Hamilton Street that, over the past decade, have together managed to make old Yaletown new again. Young and trendy, anyway. Step inside the Blue Water and settle in at the bar at happy hour and you will see that the restaurant was conceived with the philosophy that sustenance includes entertainment. There are always at least four bartenders rushing this way and that, working blenders, filling ice buckets, and performing an occasional percussive dance with their cocktail shakers, in a well-orchestrated assault on the impressive local thirst. Farther down the bar the grey-haired Yoshihiro Tabo works a less frenetic but equally productive pace, turning out platter after platter of sushi, sashimi, and nigiri rolls. And directly opposite, across the 170-seat dining room, which is filling fast, Pabst can be found directing his front kitchen crew of seven, already pumping out plates in a steady rhythm. And if, like the contemporary sports fan or concertgoer, you prefer your action enlarged and once removed on the JumboTron instead of live and real, flat-screen televisions mounted around the room run closed-circuit broadcasts from each workstation.

Since the day it opened in 2003, the Blue Water has been a perennial favourite in the seafood category in all of the Vancouver restaurant rankings. Even today it remains entrenched at the top, whether you consult the establishment press (*Vancouver Magazine*), the alternative media (*Georgia Straight*), or even the mouthpiece of the more-expensive-the-better Americans (*Robb Report*). And this has been accomplished above all else by virtue of culinary merit in a place of a scale that dictates you should least expect it. Add the seats on the terrace, the private rooms, and the bar to those in the main dining room and the tally can reach three hundred diners at one seating. There is no confusing the place with a seafood shrine like Éric Ripert's three-Michelin-starred Le Bernardin in Manhattan, but the Blue Water aims for a broader significance. In short, they are constantly trying to solve the riddle of how to properly select seafood on the basis of its sustainability without letting all this environmental due diligence get in the way of a good nosh-up.

All good contemporary chefs and restaurateurs must wrestle with the same conundrum. But smaller, chef-driven haute cuisine restaurants have a far easier job of it. They attract a trusting clientele, eager to learn and be led someplace new. That experience is part of what the customer is paying for. So too is the idea that the expensive day-boat Chatham cod or Ipswich clams they are eating taste better and more exclusive only when they inconveniently run out mid-service. More than one old Montreal waiter has told me a story—regrettably impossible to confirm—that back in the eighties, in the early days of the wonderful and ridiculously expensive seafood emporium Milos, on Avenue du Parc, that they used to pretend to run out of things all the time, and then whip the customers into an ordering frenzy by having a waiter yell out from the kitchen door, "The truck from Fulton's finally here! We've got more swordfish!" They would capitalize on the ensuing excitement by swiftly selling out a big fish that had been sitting on ice in the kitchen all day.

Times change, and big, smooth-running showpiece restaurants like Blue Water are not supposed to run out of things nowadays. Their varied selection of irreproachably fresh seafood is expected to be immune to the vagaries of supply. And in B.C., where conservationism runs relatively strong, and they are all too aware of what happened to the east coast fisheries for Atlantic cod, bluefin tuna, Atlantic salmon, and skate—to name just a few—customers also expect that every wild fish on the menu be conscientiously sourced and the cultivated ones be responsibly farmed. These guidelines are tricky in a place where the occasionally myopic local outlook has it that even farmed fish such as nice, nutritious, and inexpensive Atlantic salmon is a strike against the planet rather than for it. So out of necessity, the Blue Water plays it safe: every type of fish, shellfish, and mollusc that makes an appearance on its long menus—from the raw bar to the sushi bar to the main dining room—comes with a stamp of approval for consumption from Ocean Wise, the conservation program launched by the Vancouver Aquarium, or Seafood Watch, the Monterey Aquarium's program that inspired it, or Sea Choice, or some other similarly respected watchdog.

Commendable as that is, it does not always make for the most exciting dining choices. Start your dinner there with oysters and you will find that although the list is twenty-strong, all of them are farmed and most are west coast sourced. Over at the sushi bar, Tabo is licensed in Japan to slice and serve the highly poisonous *fugu*, but hereabouts he focuses his lovely knifework and restrained inventiveness on benign local species like salmon and tuna, along with a few predictable farmed imports like *hamachi*. Pabst, meanwhile, works largely with local Dungeness crab, trap-caught (never dredged) prawns, ahi, and albacore (but never bluefin or even yellowfin) tuna, local halibut, local scallops, all varieties of wild local salmon, farmed (inland) white sturgeon, and of course wild sablefish (aka Alaskan black cod) from B.C. and Alaska.

The last is so popular now, and its market penetration so entrenched across North America, that it is difficult to remember that it was largely unheard of here not so long ago. In early 2001, I was in Boston to attend a James Beard dinner with Susur Lee at Ken Oringer's excellent restaurant Clio, which is in the Eliot Hotel, alongside the Harvard Club on Commonwealth Avenue. The evening before the event, starting around midnight, Oringer and his chefs put on a post-service dinner for all the visiting chefs—such as Lee, Doug Rodriguez, Julian Serrano, and many others. And at about 2 A.M., when we were about halfway through his twenty-five-odd courses, Ming Tsai turned up from his restaurant Blue Ginger, in Wellesley, and announced he had a problem that he needed help with. "I need a new fish," he said. Blue Ginger Sea Bass had been the number-one-selling item on his menu since the day he opened four years previous. But the signature fish for his signature dish was fast being eaten into extinction; Chilean sea bass that used to be delivered to him in twenty-five-pound fillets were now turning up at ten pounds whole. "We have a duty as chefs not to sell endangered fish," Tsai told me. The consensus at the table that night was that he should try substituting Alaskan black cod. That dish became so ubiquitous within the next five years that it is almost impossible to imagine how dubious Tsai was. Especially given that the highly original Japanese chef Nobuyuki Matsuhisa—of the twenty-two-restaurant Nobu chain—had introduced miso to black cod a decade earlier. All the same, when Tsai got back to Wellesley he gave it a try. Ten years on it is still on the menu, still a bestseller, and stocks of black cod remain sound.

Things do not usually work out so well. It is easy to think of other fish like the Chilean sea bass whose popularity on the plate made them so scarce in the ocean that chefs stopped putting them on their menus altogether (invariably attempting to get good media coverage out of the decision by cloaking in freshly acquired environmental principles their refusal to pay the elevated, scarcity-driven prices). The beleaguered swordfish and bluefin tuna come readily to mind. And the last time I visited Michael Stadtländer at his Eigensinn Farm restaurant, in Singhampton, Ontario, no sooner had the champion of locavorism given me a tour of his trout pond than he disconsolately confided how much he missed cooking skate. The list of goners goes on and on. But it is harder to come up with even a handful of fish that emerged from nowhere to capture the culinary imagination quite so quickly and endur-ingly as the Alaskan black cod—and survived their new popularity to boot. Most trendy, freshly discovered fish turn out to be a flash in the pan. Tasmania's Petuna Seafoods, and the exceptional ocean trout they farm in the clean, brackish waters of the Southern Ocean, got off to a roaring start in Toronto in 2006. Then just as quickly it fell off the map, probably because locavores could not stand to eat a fish with a better air-miles account than they had. Keith Froggett, at Scaramouche, introduced me that same year to an excellent farmed Atlantic cod produced by Johnson Seafarms, off Scotland's Shetland Isles, but despite the quality of the product, the operation went dramatically bankrupt in 2008.

Other neglected curiosities such as escolar come and go, but few enjoy enduring popularity in the North American skillet.

Which is why I so like that at a mainstream, popular, and risk-averse restaurant like Blue Water, Pabst fields an entire menu of "unsung" options for those who cannot take another plate of salmon or tuna. And that furthermore, the fish featured there—from jellyfish to giant Pacific octopus, mackerel, flying squid, and sea urchin to the common sardine—are often in even better shape as a species than his mainstream offerings. Even the pleasant caviar with which he enhances some of those dishes is harvested from farm-raised shortnose sturgeon in faraway New Brunswick. That "unsung" menu may never account for more than five percent of total covers, but it plays a disproportionate role in diversifying the public taste, is good for generating media coverage, and is offered up without any objectionable environmental proselytizing. You can enjoy your meal instead of feeling worthy and dutiful and having to eat it off reclaimed wood like, say, at Eigensinn Farm. Or having to read about carbon footprints in the margin of the menu, like at others restaurants sadly too numerous to list.

Intriguingly, Pabst hails from Bavaria, where they eat wild boar for breakfast and fish usually means smoked eel or rollmops and is just a snack. He is the first chef in his family. His career began when as a teenager he took a job at a modest bistro just across the Belgian border and there, despite the simple oeuvre (chicken, sausages, frites), discovered both interest and promise. Moving up, after his German military service was complete, he decamped to Aachen, resting place of Charlemagne, to serve an apprenticeship under Christof Lang at his elegant French restaurant,

Cured Herring Tartare with Apple, Onion, and Coriander

Chef Frank Pabst

Serves 4

1/4 cup (60 mL) kosher salt
2 tbsp (30 mL) granulated sugar
4 B.C. herring, frozen, then thawed, scaled, and filleted*
1 Granny Smith apple, peeled and diced
1/4 cup (60 mL) minced red onion
2 tbsp (30 mL) sour cream
1 tbsp (15 mL) yogurt
1 tbsp (15 mL) mayonnaise
Juice of 1 lemon
1 tbsp (15 mL) coriander seeds, toasted and crushed
1 tbsp (15 mL) minced dill
1 tbsp (15 mL) minced chives
Salt and pepper
1 Granny Smith apple, julienned
1 large bunch young watercress, picked over
4 slices pumpernickel

Combine the salt and sugar with 2 cups (500 mL) cold water and bring to a boil, stirring until solids are completely dissolved. Chill the brine thoroughly. Place herring fillets in a snug container, cover with the brine, and transfer to the refrigerator for 1 hour.

Place the fillets flesh side down on a dry kitchen towel and with a very sharp knife scrape away as much of their skin as possible. Then cut the fillets into 1/4-inch (5 mm) dice and transfer to a large bowl. Add the diced apple, onion, sour cream, yogurt, mayonnaise, lemon juice, coriander, dill, and chives; mix well. Season with salt and pepper, mix again, and adjust seasonings.

Toss together the julienned apple and watercress. Divide the salad among 4 chilled plates, mound the tartare on top of the salad, and serve with a piece of pumpernickel on the side.

*It is advisable to freeze the herring to kill any parasites that might be present. You can save yourself some trouble by simply purchasing frozen fish or even frozen fillets.

La Becasse, where the cuisine was classically inspired but mildly inventive, with a solid nod to the more robust German appetite (think seared foie gras with a salad of warm potatoes and young garlic). French cuisine inspired Pabst, so when the apprenticeship was done, he headed for the south of France, where he served under such culinary luminaries as Dominique Le Stanc (when he had two Michelin stars at Chantecler, in the Hôtel Negresco in Nice), Serge Philippin (Restaurant de Bacon, one Michelin star, Antibes), Daniel Ettlinger (Le Diamant Rose, Colle-sur-Loup), and finally Jacques Chibois (La Bastide Saint-Antoine, two Michelin stars, Grasse). Each of these coastal or near-coastal restaurants specializes in the preparation of fish. The path was set.

After four years in the south of France, Pabst quit Europe for North America, heading first to San Francisco, where he knocked on doors from Chez Panisse on down, to no avail. The noted Alsatian chef Hubert Keller (Fleur de Lys) was the only *patron* to even ask Pabst for his CV, and in the end he did not offer a job, just some advice on which work papers he was missing. In 1994 Pabst finally ended up with a gig at the old Chartwell restaurant in the Four Seasons Vancouver. Two years later, he moved to join chef Rob Feenie at Lumière in those early, exciting days when it was first making the transition to tasting-menu-only format. Feenie made him sous-chef, and then chef de cuisine, and then in 1999, Pabst set out with front-of-house business partner John Blakely to open Bistro Pastis. It promptly collected the gold award for best new restaurant in the annual *Vancouver Magazine* restaurant awards. But the partnership with Blakely was not destined to last. With children on the horizon, Pabst next moved to the relative economic security of Jack Evrensel's Top Table restaurant group, whose number includes an enviable list of the best restaurants in B.C.: West and CinCin, in Vancouver, and Araxi, in Whistler.

Pabst has been executive chef at the Blue Water Café since 2003. It was his first big restaurant, and he admits that he initially found its scale daunting. So he simplified his ideas a little until he found a comfort zone where he could once again add complexity to his plates. A decade has passed. And with that, as he concluded his story over a lunch of hand-cut noodles at the Sha Lin Noodle House on West Broadway, he laid down his chopsticks and we set off for his car. For Pabst had offered to take me to see his main fish supplier, Albion Fisheries, on Great Northern Way. There are no small day-boat fish markets in Vancouver; the best fish comes from too far afield. Big restaurants all order from big suppliers like this one.

"Albion is such a big supplier. They're interested in sustain-ability because they want to sell and keep selling," Pabst said on the drive there. As he explained, the process of selecting fish responsibly has been made relatively easy, courtesy of the readily accessible research from organizations like Ocean Wise. "Whenever we see a new product, we just give them a call. But it's not like there are that many new products out there, and it's not like it used to be. Now, when a supplier brings me something new, they want me to know exactly where it comes from, and how they get it, so along with the sample, they hand me a CD-ROM."

The scale of Albion was shocking. The tour began in a corporate boardroom where we were equipped with hairnets, hard hats, white coats, and a twenty-seven-page product list. And then via a circuitous route across the order floor, we made our way downstairs to the processing plant, entering through the shellfish section, where tubs of Atlantic lobsters and blue crabs were stacked twenty or thirty feet high. Next we came across a series of rooms where elderly Chinese workers sat hunched over tables shelling freshly boiled shrimp. Then we passed stacked boxes of ahi tuna, mako shark, and escolar, that virtual tub of butter with fins (the fish so oily that its consumption is banned in some countries, its portion size limited in others, for fear of its lubricating effect on the digestive system). Next we came upon towers of boxes of black cod and Arctic char. Everything was frozen or cooked or both.

Our last stop, beyond an ice-encased doorway, was a freezer room that stood four storeys tall. Here was the previous summer's salmon run—sockeye, chinook, and coho, filleted, skinned, and crusted with ice. The storage boxes were stacked to the ceiling and went off in every which direction, like a deep-freeze version of the government warehouse in the closing sequence of *Raiders of the Lost Ark*. Reading about quota numbers of thousand of tonnes of fish in the newspaper is one thing; seeing some large part of it stacked up neatly in boxes is quite another. The scale of the kill is awesome. And it made me think that whatever Ocean Wise says, I had better take my son Max fishing out in the Queen Charlottes sooner rather than later. I would have preferred to take him fly-fishing on the east coast like my father did with me—but of course, those salmon are gone.

~ 4 ~

FOIE GRAS

According to the culinary gospel of chef Normand Laprise, a restaurant freezer is suited to storing berries in their seasonal prime, ice cream, and sorbet but nothing more—not even a tub of *fond blanc* or demi-glace—and so his menu at Toqué! in Montreal is vulnerable to the vagaries of market and season more than any other I know. There is, however, one item listed on it that has not changed a whit since that happy day back in 1993 that Toqué! first opened its doors on Rue Saint-Denis. Price aside, it did not change through the subsequent renovations that saw the original street-front kitchen move downstairs, or the expansion into an adjacent space that saw the one-time forty-seat restaurant grow to accommodate sixty and then eighty diners. And it was still on the menu after 2004, when Toqué! decamped to an all-new and far more spacious site on Place Jean-Paul-Riopelle. So it now seems safe to say that as long as there is a Toqué! there will be *foie gras chaud "fraîchement Toqué!"*

"What is *foie gras chaud 'fraîchement Toqué!'*?" I asked the waiter when I first spotted it on the menu 1993.

"'*Fraîchement Toqué!*' means the inspiration of the chef," he replied. "It's what he feels like doing."

"And what does he feel like doing tonight?"

"I don't know," the waiter said, with a smile and a shrug. "Chef changes his mind all the time."

This was intriguing. The word *toqué* is not to be confused with *toque*, the name for the tall, formal pleated paper hat once favoured by French chefs. Add an accent to the hat and you get something completely different: a patois expression that means, well, crazy. So, if you want to know what *foie gras chaud "fraîchement Toqué!"* means and the chef is too mad to tell anyone about it, you have no choice but to order it. And while I do not remember exactly how Laprise did it that night twenty years ago, I do recall the moment, vividly, right down to where I was sitting in the restaurant and who I was with, because the experience was so very poignant. The table was near the back of the room, I was dining with my mother—and at first bite it suddenly struck home for the first time that I had endured a deprived childhood. Twenty-five years on earth and I had never yet tasted hot seared foie gras! Mercifully there had been foie gras terrines aplenty, and naturally, plenty of foie gras mousse too, but I had never experienced the stuff in its hot, glorious apotheosis, with its melted fat coursing luxuriously over my tongue bite after bite so exquisitely that medium-fat smoked meat would forever after seem like melba toast. Those first two perfectly seared hot slabs of the exquisite stuff set me off on a whole new life course. And ever since, I have wanted to know what *foie gras chaud "fraîchement Toqué!"* might be at any particular moment pretty much continuously.

So I keep checking whenever I can. Thus I can tell you authoritatively that Laprise has of late been preoccupied with saucing his seared foie gras with the light, fruity, and mildly acidic counterbalance of pear water. Picture, for example, a thick slice of hot foie gras in a pool of the liquid studded with halved ground cherries, small cubes of jellied honey, braised baby turnips, and at the side of the plate a small heap of seasoning—salt mixed with sugar, powdered citrus, and sumac—left to the diner to apply according to taste. Another recent time pear jelly, hazelnut oil, and begonia petals made their way into the equation. Another time Laprise ran with sliced poached pear, small Quebec-sourced morels, and a sprinkling of crumbled toasted pistachios. I remember lentils once appearing on the plate. I could go on and on.

But all that now matters of his preparation in 1993 is that back then, while other chefs across the country sensible enough to be cooking with foie gras were still turning to major foreign producers like France and Hungary, Laprise was instead using homegrown product from what was then a nascent Quebec industry. Palmex, in Carignan, which has been the favoured Toqué! supplier for more than a decade, was not founded until 1998. Le Canard Goulu, in Saint-Apollinaire, which is the preferred source for the finest restaurants in Quebec City, did not open for business until 1997. In 1993 Annette and Élisé François, future founders of Aux Champs d'Élisé, of Marieville, were then just experimenting with moulard ducks as a sideline to their dairy farm. Of all the big

Quebec players in the foie gras industry, only Élevages Périgord was open for business when Laprise started serving fresh foie gras at his restaurant. But the fledgling Quebec industry that Laprise worked so hard to promote now produces two hundred tons of foie gras a year—roughly one percent of world supply—and much of it is of such high quality that it is favoured by innumerable top chefs stateside, among them Thomas Keller, Daniel Boulud, and Mario Batali. Even Charlie Trotter preferred it—before he went over to the dark side and stopped serving foie gras in 2002. They all correctly recognize the corn-fed Quebec product to be superior to its rice-mash-fattened cousin from New York State, whether its purpose is to be seared, salt-cured, made into a terrine, incorporated into a mousse, cooked sous-vide, grilled, roasted whole à la Eckart Witzigmann, or what have you.

One of the worst things about being a restaurant critic is all those restaurants people heartily recommend to you that turn out to be really awful. Breaking the news can be awkward. Enduring the meal to prove your point of view is akin to torture. So that very rare occasion when a new restaurant actually lives up to its advance billing is a singularly happy occasion. Surpassing what has been promised is all but unheard of. But one glorious evening back in the winter of 2001, this happened to me not once, but twice in the same evening.

I was in Vancouver. I had an eight o'clock reservation for Rob Feenie's Lumière, a first visit there that would ultimately lead to me eating at least a dozen courses and staggering off to my hotel convinced that I had just eaten at the best restaurant in the country. The extraordinary thing about that evening was that I had almost cancelled, because I did not want to leave the restaurant I had visited right beforehand, where I had met a friend for pre-dinner cocktails, been talked into a quick snack, and after a single taste decided it was impossible that I could do any better across town. That restaurant was Vancouver restaurateur Jack Evrensel's Ouest (which later became West, so as to stop confusing the locals). The chef was David Hawksworth, who was then freshly repatriated from the U.K. and hereabouts unknown. The dish he had put in front of me was an early version of something you still find on his menu today at his eponymous Hawksworth Restaurant, at the Rosewood Hotel Georgia: parfait of Quebec foie gras and chicken livers with apple jelly.

The dish was flawless, from the thinness of the pork back fat that wrapped the parfait, to its texture, to the temperature at which it was served, to its hue, which was uniform from centre to edge, without the faintest trace of oxidation, as if the slice had just been cut from a freshly opened terrine. Which was impossible, because it was glued to the plate by a shallow pool of set apple jelly. Looking back now, after having happily eaten so much more of Hawksworth's food, I realize that this one dish handily encapsulated his culinary philosophy—which, simply put, is built on a foundation of impeccable European training, but rendered contemporary with a deft, lightening rethink and a colourful presentation. When you have that plate these days at Hawksworth, the jelly is from green apple, edible flowers enliven the picture, and a tuft of foie gras candyfloss sits off to one side. But never mind the trimmings; it was the mousse or parfait that had moved me, so I followed up with a little investigation as to where Hawksworth had picked up the recipe.

To begin at the beginning, Hawksworth was born in Vancouver to English parents who shortly afterwards went their separate ways. His childhood was punctuated by a number of moves back and forth across the pond. At the tender age of six, Hawksworth became the first pupil in the history of his primary school in York, England, to be allowed to leave the premises at lunchtime for the more salubrious offerings of home. It would be appealing to put this down to the child's precociously refined palate, but alas, the facts are different: "I hated the school. It was so archaic, so regimented. I had culture shock. I refused to eat the food." Both Hawksworth's mother and maternal grandmother were good cooks, making everything from scratch. His uncle Clive was a professional chef, at the Connaught Rooms, a posh banquet facility on Great Queen Street in Covent Garden. "He was a very charismatic, interesting guy," Hawksworth recalls. "I remember visiting him there once and he said to me, 'Would you like something to eat?' He brought me this beef tenderloin and I sat and ate in his office. I'll never forget that piece of beef." It had been dry-aged to meltingly tender and flavour-intensifying perfection. Back in Vancouver, as a young teenager in search of a summer job, Hawksworth did as so many kids do and turned to the restaurant industry, washing dishes in a fish-and-chip shop. Soon enough, his responsibilities included peeling potatoes. One thing led to another: when he left high school, well aware that "he couldn't sit still in an office," he returned instinctively to what he knew, but this time secured a position in a proper kitchen—at the Beach House in Stanley Park. Hawksworth warmed to the marginal eccentricity of the kitchen staff and he enjoyed the absence of routine. "Every day was different." Surrounded by real chefs, he soon aspired to join their ranks. He made inquiries about cooking school but deemed that "too expensive." Chef Frank Abbinante told his young commis to pursue a proper apprenticeship.

His first was at Le Crocodile, under the esteemed Michel Jacob, godfather of French cuisine in Vancouver. Umberto Menghi fulfilled the same leading role for local Italian cuisine, and so Hawksworth took on apprenticeships at a pair of his kitchens, too (lunches at Settebello followed by dinners at Il Giardino). And he rounded out the week with weekend shifts at the venerable Villa del Lupo. "I was running around, working around four jobs, but they were all part-time." Then he quit them all for an opportunity in Tofino, on the west coast of Vancouver Island, where Menghi's long-time corporate chef Ron Lammie was setting up the Orca Lodge. Hawksworth saw Tofino as a stepping stone, a small town where it was easy to live cheaply and save money. "Everywhere I had worked, they did the same garnishes for everything. They cooked the same chicken and veal." He had already discovered that things were very different elsewhere, courtesy of two recently acquired cookbooks—Raymond Blanc's *Recipes from Le Manoir aux Quat' Saisons*, published in 1988, and Marco Pierre White's groundbreaking *White Heat*, published in 1990. "When I looked at what I was doing and opened those two books, it was quite, um, *different.* The recipes, the finesse, the number of things on the plate … it looked like they were working on a different planet." It took him ten months in Tofino to save (just) enough money to move to planet England to undertake his real training.

Hawksworth arrived in London in November 1991, preceded by only a week by two letters of application: one to Blanc at Le Manoir aux Quat' Saisons, in Great Milton, Oxfordshire, and the other to White at Harveys, in Wandsworth, London. Each chef had two Michelin stars and was swamped with job applicants, but Hawksworth got lucky. White had just opened a second restaurant, The Canteen, in Chelsea Harbour, a relatively large and casual venture that was a smash hit from the get-go, and he was desperate for staff.

"I had one contact in London," Hawksworth recounts. "I landed, I phoned this family friend, and she said, 'Marco called. He wants you to come by Canteen.'" Hawksworth arrived in England on a Saturday and started work on Monday, jet-lagged, disoriented, and a half-hour late for his eight-in-the-morning shift on the fish station. The new chef poissonier lacked experience, local or otherwise. "It was a big restaurant and it was incredibly busy—so busy that we had to start buying fish broken down instead of whole because we didn't have time to fillet them anymore. So we'd have portion-sized pieces of turbot and brill in the fridge and someone would yell for one and I had no idea which was which. Everyone else there seemed to have come from two- and three-[Michelin-]star kitchens. I felt like I had skipped eight years [of training]." But he muddled through and got the hang of things—new things—from eight in the morning till one in the morning, six days a week and sometimes more. One day in the fourth month, to his considerable relief, he got a call from the office of Raymond Blanc offering a job interview.

When the appointed day finally came, Hawksworth had worked fourteen days straight. "I was bagged." Still, nervous, he slept for only three hours, and then got up to wait for the minicab that was supposed to take him from his flat in Southfields to the train station. The driver got lost and Hawksworth missed the first train to Oxford. By the time he finally arrived there, he was in a panic. He hopped into the tidiest-looking minicab in the queue and set off up the M40. "We drove on and on and finally cut through some country village and in a curve started to drift into the oncoming lane, and I'm thinking, 'We must be getting ready to turn but where's the Manoir?" No Manoir, but there was an oncoming car—Hawksworth's driver was fast asleep.

"I flew head-first into the front foot well and my feet were sticking up in the air. There was glass and blood everywhere. I was taken away strapped to a board. When I woke up that night in the hospital, I phoned Canteen to say that I couldn't make it the next day and they clearly thought I was doing a runner." As it happened, he did not quit The Canteen for another month, not until a second and far more agreeable excursion to Oxfordshire ended in his passing Blanc's customary test—*take zese three eggs, make me sabayon, cook for me zese rouget*—and being offered a job as chef de partie.

Hawksworth spent four years working for Blanc, first making the jump to sous-chef at Le Manoir and next, in mid-1996, becoming executive chef for Blanc's next project, a 150-seat brasserie in central Oxford called Le Petit Blanc. (Since renamed Brasserie Blanc, it spawned a national chain that is now eight restaurants strong and growing.) His quest for experience continued apace: later that year he returned to London to become head chef at the Soho institution L'Escargot, handily maintaining its Michelin star for eighteen months before moving on to work at Philip Howard's The Square, in St. James's (which later packed up its two Michelin stars and decamped to Mayfair). His next move of consequence was to join the huge kitchen staff young Michelin-starred chef Bruno Loubet was assembling for London restaurateur Oliver Peyton's £3.8-million Italian-themed flagship in Knightsbridge, Isola. Hawksworth had by then worked for or with nearly all the young chefs who were wresting the attention of the international gourmand from its traditional playground of France, and in the process leading the world. As it always does, haute cuisine has changed again since.

"Food was *bigger* then. It was less product-driven. It was more about how many different components you could get onto the plate. Some of it was too complex. Some of it was ... perfect." Hawksworth looks on those sometime culinary mentors as having possessed different strengths. "Marco—his flavours were clean and perfect. And he was a technician. You wanted to bone out a pig's trotter? He could do it faster and better than anyone on the planet. He was very gifted technically." Hawksworth confirms Raymond Blanc's reputation for having a far different and far more cerebral skill set: "Blanc's palate, when it came to acidity and texture, and how we look at colours, and how to balance it all—he was very, very good at that."

His management style was different, too. Where White was aggressive, often abusive, and known to get into the occasional fist fight (often with his young protégé Gordon Ramsay), Blanc preferred mind games. As Blanc himself remarked to *The Times* of London in 2008, he believes that "under pressure and sometimes fear, people grow the best." Hawksworth summarizes the Blanc experience like so: "You've seen *The Office* with Ricky Gervais? Let's just say I can't watch it. It's too familiar ... Blanc is very talented, but his main goal was to fuck you up." Often this seems to be the norm in the Michelin-starred European kitchen, but Hawksworth found an exception in Philip Howard. "Phil is a *normal* person. Very articulate. If you met him on the street, there is no way you would think he was a chef. Phil was an inspiration because he was down to earth even with what he achieved. I built a lot of confidence there."

The year of relative calm at The Square was followed by utter chaos under Loubet at Isola, an architectural extravaganza spread over two floors, with space for 250 diners under its Murano chandeliers. "It was supposed to be this über-Italian experience. Anybody who even *looked* Italian got hired as a waiter. We ended up with fifty Italians, forty gypsies, and ten Croats." They also went through five managers in the first couple of months. Chefs were showing up to work irretrievably sloshed; Hawksworth remembers one chopping unwashed parsley with the edge of a spatula while he tried to wake the poissonier because seven branzino were on fire in his wood-burning oven. When Jack Evrensel rang from Vancouver to try to lure Hawksworth home, he had worked thirty days straight. It took a few more calls, but in the end Evrensel came through with the magic number. Not the salary, but the seats: the new restaurant on Granville Street would have just seventy-four.

Which brings us back to that foie gras and chicken liver parfait. In haute cuisine, foie gras parfait or mousse was traditionally deployed as a luxurious binding agent for the most sophisticated of terrines. For example, in 2003, when Marc Thuet was the executive chef at The Fifth, he served me the finest, most elaborate terrine I have ever eaten. It had three layers, with breast of woodcock on one level, a little breast of wild Scottish pheasant on the next, and a breast of partridge down below. The first and second layers were divided by a strip of sliced black truffle, and the second and third by sliced black trumpet mushrooms. The breasts of fowl—which were of course oval because they had been cut crosswise when the terrine was sliced—were lightly cooked and set, floating in foie gras mousse. Foie gras mousse that, as it happened, tasted almost identical to Hawksworth's, because the recipe shared the same lineage.

Thuet picked it up in the 1980s when he put in occasional shifts at Pierre Koffmann's much-missed three-Michelin-star restaurant La Tante Claire, in Chelsea. There, Koffmann made a three-tiered terrine with breast of pheasant, squab, and teal. Among the chefs in Koffmann's employ was a young Éric Chavot (who would eventually earn two Michelin stars at The Capital, in Knightsbridge). After Tante Claire, Chavot went to work for Marco Pierre White at Harveys. There, White always featured a dish of hot seared foie gras. And, of course, even though fatty duck livers are bloated, misshapen things, packing one lobe twice the size of the other, White would serve nothing but perfectly proportioned escalopes. This translated into a lot of foie gras trimmings, and that is very expensive waste. What to do? Chavot suggested a parfait of foie gras, all on its own, adorned only with *gelée de Sauternes* or perhaps one made with truffle or Madeira.

"So I made a golden apple jelly to lighten it up and make the dish—if possible—lighter," Hawksworth explained to me many years later. "The rest is history."

On their most festive occasions, the Chinese of Fujian Province turn to a ridiculously elaborate dish called Buddha Jumps Over the Wall, which at its most authentic features some twenty different types of meat, from shark's fin, abalone, and sea cucumber to dried scallops, pigs' trotters, lamb fillets, a whole duck, a whole chicken, and a sizeable portion of cured ham. The joke implicit in the name is obviously that Buddha is resolutely vegetarian; the idea is that the aroma of this dish is so divinely alluring that even the Buddha would jump over a wall just to get at it. And that is what I was thinking about on November 18, 2005, in the kitchen at Lumière restaurant in Vancouver, as I watched Charlie Trotter nibble contentedly on one of chef Rob Feenie's exquisite pheasant *boudins blancs*.

Feenie had served them earlier that night drizzled with rich veal jus and plated on a bed of orzo as one of the courses on the two chefs' elaborate $1,000-per-plate tasting menu conceived to celebrate the tenth anniversary of Lumière. The thing was that Trotter was then very much in the news as the most prominent chef to support a PETA-proposed city-wide ban on the consumption of foie gras in his hometown of Chicago. He had taken foie gras off his menu three years before. I had just spent fifteen minutes unavailingly attempting to convince him of the salubrious living conditions of Quebec's foie gras–producing moulard ducks. (Despite the martinis and much wine, I had stopped shy of humouring Marc Thuet's request when he heard where I was going—"You see Trotter, kick him in the balls for me!") And now here was Trotter reaching for yet another delicate little *boudin*. It did not say so on the menu, but you would have to have a palate immeasurably inferior to that of the ten-time James Beard award–winning chef to not recognize that Feenie had laced his pheasant heavily with you-know-what.

"Mmm," Trotter said. "It tastes a little of liver."

Yes, I'll say. That's how good Feenie's pheasant-and-foie-gras *boudin* taste: you could call them PETA Jumps Over the Wall. Some years later I finally talked Feenie into giving me the recipe for them. But the fact is that they are such a nuisance to put together that the recipe serves largely to remind one of why we go to restaurants in the first place. The recipe for the foie gras parfait of Éric Chavot's is less complicated, but it is time consuming, and there is no way to make less than an entire terrine. In my experience having that in your fridge is highly impractical and not at all good for your health. I have only made it once. And I have the same reservations about investing the time required into making a terrine of foie gras entier—which is to say an even more luxurious terrine of pure, unadulterated foie gras. I learned to make Mark McEwan's singular layered interpretation, which he developed in the 1990s for his menu restaurant North 44, fielded to general acclaim at James Beard House in New York, and sentenced me to test out and write up as a recipe of domestically reasonable, non-restaurant proportions for his first cookbook, *Great Food at Home*, which I co-authored. I designed it for a single terrine, but even so the recipe requires two entire foies gras, involves several stages spread out over several days, and in the end delivers a quantity of terrine that—even after I gave half of it away for Christmas—I was still eating six months later. It was great to learn the trick of it, but when all you need and want is one thick slice, you really are better off buying just that. Yet long before we worked on that cookbook together, McEwan taught me a different foie gras recipe that to this day I find indispensable. And it is quick and easy, too.

McEwan grew up on meat and potatoes in Buffalo, New York, where his father, a crooner (who got a callback for *Oklahoma!*), had moved to perform on local live radio. "He sounded too much like Sinatra for his own good," McEwan remarked dryly to me once. "When you sound like Frank Sinatra but you're not Frank Sinatra, you're just another lounge singer." At sixteen, Mark took a job at a popular Buffalo restaurant called Mindy's Wine Cellar. It was not an interest in the food industry that drew him there. "I needed a job and I got a job," McEwan said. His initial summer-long encounter with the restaurant industry was not an appealing one: he made $1.65 an hour as a dishwasher. The days were long and the owners obsessive—at least about the state of his dish pit at the end of his shift. They would check the corners; they would lift the drain cover out of the floor and check that, too; satisfied or not, they did not offer a discount on staff meals. "There was no way I was going to work all day at that just to give a third of my wage back for dinner." So young McEwan got by on the most intact dinner rolls he could find on cleared-away plates. At the end of a shift, after a few drinks, there was always the promise of the Mighty Taco, on Delaware Avenue. "It was a drive-through, and you put your money in a square hole in the wall and the food came out." He favoured the spicy bean burrito; it has no connection, however nascent, to the lobster, avocado, and jicama taco that would turn up on the menu at North 44 twenty years later. One night Mindy's was short a cook, and the manager, a young blond woman who drove a powder-blue AMC Pacer with a white vinyl roof and matching upholstery, asked Mark if he would take a place on the line. He did, and he liked it.

By then, McEwan's father was working in television production at Buffalo's Channel 4. But this was the mid-seventies, cable television was making its first serious incursion into the traditional broadcast market, and the elder McEwan was offered a job with better prospects in Toronto. The McEwan family moved north. When Mark finished Grade 13, he took a job on the line at a restaurant called the Country Squire, on the highway near Oakville. His intention was to enrol in hotel management at the University of Guelph, but he wanted to work for a year first. Looking to broaden his experience, he filled out countless job applications at Toronto hotels, unavailingly, until a family connection put him in the interview chair opposite Swiss executive chef Joseph Vonlanthen at the now defunct Constellation Hotel, near

Pearson International Airport. "He liked the fact that I wore a tie to the interview," McEwan recalls. Vonlanthen had impeccable training, but unlike so many of his countrymen, he did not adhere to the European tradition of long, rigorous training and slow promotions; he rewarded enthusiasm unconditionally. In 1976, McEwan started as an apprentice on the line; one year later he was a chef de station. By now he was no longer interested in management and the front of the house: "All the action was in the kitchen." In 1977, he enrolled at George Brown College; two years later he graduated with two internships under his belt and moved on to the Grand National Hotel in Lucerne, where he served as commis de cuisine. He savoured the culinary side of the European equation, but was turned off by the poor wages and an obvious lack of upward mobility. It was not his dream to become a "forty-year-old sous-chef with a one-bedroom apartment and a mattress on the floor."

Good call. After six months, he returned to the Constellation and, two years later at age twenty-two, was made sous-chef. Then he quit the distant suburbs for the allure of downtown and what was then de facto film festival headquarters and one of the top hotels in the country, the Sutton Place. At twenty-three, executive sous-chef McEwan cooked for Pope John Paul II; at twenty-four he was made executive chef and became—and remains—the youngest chef in the country to ever hold such a position at a major hotel. The salary was good but, in a now familiar pattern, he soon moved on for a different challenge: in 1985, aged twenty-eight, he quit in favour of running his own place, and with two business partners purchased Pronto from restaurateur Franco Prevedello.

It was the first time McEwan had taken charge of the kitchens of a fine-dining establishment with just eighty seats, and he excelled. (For what it's worth, I vividly recall the highlight of my first meal there as a teenager: a large, succulent, and implausibly tasty beef tenderloin, charred but rare, topped with poached veal marrow and drizzled with a pure, veal-enriched reduction.) The restaurant swiftly established itself as one of the very best in town; not so the relations between the business triumvirate. In 1989, on Yonge Street a few blocks north of Eglinton, McEwan finally found a location to build a place that he would call his own and focused his attention there instead. The next spring he opened North 44.

"I had a budget of $700,000 and I spent two million—what a genius," McEwan said of the venture eighteen years on. "One reason was a total lack of experience in construction. I had too much enthusiasm. I rebuilt the entire building and I didn't even own it. I almost sank my ship."

North 44 opened in May 1990. The recession arrived a few months later. McEwan owed contractors; he owed suppliers; he got further and further behind. "The last thing you can do is go back to the bank to say you have a problem." He didn't. "I cashed in my RRSPs. I sold my share of Pronto. I got some money—no need to say from whom, but I would have lost my fingers if I hadn't paid it back." He did that by hunkering down and working ridiculously long days. The restaurant was busy, and looking back, he admits he let it be busier than it should have been, sacrificing service to the need for numbers. By day, he made prepared foods and a line of North 44 breads. "I was up at six each morning, my car weighed down with product to sell." He started a catering business. The tide eventually turned: by decade's end, North 44 was a perennial top-ten finisher in *Toronto Life* magazine and had been anointed the best restaurant in town by Zagat and by *Gourmet* magazine for three years running. McEwan's wheels were no longer good for transporting baguettes around town; he was now getting around in a new Porsche 911, and what's more, he had the temerity to stop working the line each night and spend some time with his family instead. When he started talking about opening a new restaurant downtown, *Globe and Mail* restaurant critic Joanne Kates rang him up at North 44 to ask why he would do such a thing when he couldn't be behind both stoves at the same time—making it clear that this was where he was expected to stay.

"McEwan's not really a chef—he's a businessman," one chef said to me at the time.

"He just got lucky on the stock market," another said to me.

"Bymark is just going to steal business from his place uptown," one restaurateur predicted.

"*Si Bymark ne fonction pas—c'est bye-bye, Mark!*" another chef remarked gleefully.

Three of those four chefs are no longer in business. Meanwhile, Bymark is still going strong. McEwan followed that with One, a $3-million restaurant that anchors the Hazelton Hotel, where he exceeded his budgeted sales predictions for its first year by fifty percent and has annual sales considerably over $10 million. And one sunny August between opening that and following with his next venture, a $5.6-million, twenty-thousand-square-foot fine-food emporium called McEwan, in the Shops at Don Mills, he hopped into his Mercedes AMG, loaded up the trunk with tomatoes ripened in his vegetable garden on Georgian Bay, USDA Prime steaks aged for Bymark, a whole Quebec foie gras, and Cuban cigars, amongst other staples, ripped up the 401 to the province of Quebec, and followed the 40 and the 10 to Austin, on Lake Memphremagog, in the Eastern Townships, where I was taking a summer vacation with my mother, Florence.

So I got my first and only risotto lesson on the AGA, a stove McEwan had never seen or heard of before, and was obviously taken with, proclaiming its heat plate to be the best heat source for making risotto that he had ever worked on. But it was the course that preceded the grilled steaks with squash risotto that had made the deepest impression. "This would be perfect for roasting the foie gras," McEwan had said to me that afternoon, after I gave him the lowdown on the AGA's roasting oven. My interest was definitely piqued. Roast whole foie gras? Why hadn't I thought of that? McEwan apparently had not thought of it either—he attributed the recipe to the incomparable Austrian chef Eckart Witzigmann, who changed the course of European cooking in the late 1970s with his three-Michelin-star Munich restaurant Aubergine, and shortly thereafter was proclaimed a "chef of the century" by the *Guide Gault-Millau* (joining Paul Bocuse, Joël Robuchon, and Frédy Girardet in a club of four). The recipe is easy. And while in writing the recipe for this book I ventured that it would serve six to eight, be advised that McEwan, my mother, and I polished it off between the three of us, then ate the steaks and risotto, too—although I cannot say that it did much for my snooker game that night.

"Mark can come any time," my mother said as he drove off the next day.

Whole Roasted Foie Gras

Chef Mark McEwan

Serves 6 to 8

1 fresh whole foie gras, about 1-1/2 lb (675 g)
Salt and white pepper
2 tbsp (30 mL) olive oil
3 cloves garlic, peeled
2 sprigs thyme
1 sprig sage

Suggested accompaniments: sliced baguette drizzled with olive oil, seasoned
with salt and pepper, and toasted; braised wedges of apple or peach; roasted
garlic

Preheat oven to 450°F (230°C).

Place the cold foie gras on the chopping block flat side down. Use a sharp knife
to score the domed top, cutting more deeply (about 1/2 inch or 1 cm) into
the larger lobe of the liver. Season it very generously all over with salt and white
pepper. Heat a skillet on medium-high. Add the olive oil and then the foie gras,
rounded side down, moving it around in the pan with tongs so as to brown
the top all over—about 2 minutes. Flip the foie gras onto its flat side, add
the garlic, thyme, and sage to the skillet, and transfer to the oven for about
7 minutes, basting frequently. Remove skillet (do not turn off the oven), drain
off most of the fat, cover with foil, and leave to rest for about 7 minutes.
Remove the foil and return to oven for about 5 minutes, basting frequently and
draining fat as necessary.* Transfer foie gras to a warm platter with the braised
fruit, roasted garlic, and toast, and tuck in with delirious abandon.

*For cooking times, assume a total of about 16 minutes for a 1-pound liver to about
25 minutes for a 2-pound liver.

~ 5 ~

GAME

Shortly before Christmas 2011, eight lucky Toronto men converged on an excellent restaurant on Queen Street West with their minds set on the pursuit of the sort of sophisticated but essential pleasures that all levels of Canadian government do their best to prevent. No, there were no opiates on hand. And yes, all the waitresses were fully clothed and very much expected to remain that way. The contentious issue was rather about the comestibles destined for the plate. Because unlike the vast bulk of meat and fish legally consumed in this country, the stuff selected for this meal had not been sourced from dodgy intensive farms, where the miserable creatures were pumped full of drugs to prevent their getting chronically ill from their cramped and insalubrious conditions. Instead, they came from *the Canadian wild*. And to complicate matters further, the game in question was not going to be mangled by some country bumpkin who thinks that real Canadian cooking involves braising some chopped-up caribou leg in a bottle of Pepsi. Rather, it was going to be prepared by one of our finest chefs, a master with game, and a man justifiably accustomed to being well remunerated for his services. Needless to say, we have many laws on the books to protect us from this kind of thing.

For starters, in this Toronto version of a conundrum that plays out similarly all across the country, any chef who tries to sell his customers local game will be blocked by the Ontario Ministry of Natural Resources, which forbids hunting for profit—and thus the purchase or sale of locally sourced wild game meats. If they try to bypass that problem by instead sourcing game from a foreign jurisdiction and, say, importing some exquisite Scottish grouse or pheasant, they will come up against the Canadian Food Inspection Agency, which forbids imports of such tasty stuff. Regardless, the Toronto Department of Public Health forbids restaurants or food shops to sell for consumption anything caught in the wild and then processed somewhere other than a federally approved abattoir. So for the chef who wants to serve his customers a little of Canada's natural bounty, there is but one legal escape hatch: purchase game meats without a traceable receipt (i.e., through cash or contra), give it away to their customers for free, and then—nudge, nudge, wink, wink—charge them $80 for the side of carrots or bottle of water that went with it.

In the case of this dinner for eight, matters were simplified because the customer—philanthropist and truffle enthusiast Steven Latner—is also a good hunter, and had been considerate enough to shoot, kill, and provide all the required game meats himself. Furthermore, the legal dance around the billing had been long established with the chef, David Lee, co-owner of the restaurant in question, Nota Bene. For the game dinner was an annual event going back to 2005, when Lee was chef and co-owner of Splendido, on Harbord Street, which he and his partner, Yannick Bigourdan, sold in 2009. Splendido was a fine-dining restaurant, with an emphasis on Old World service, right down to little details like leather-covered purse stools that were noiselessly planted at each lady's side as they sat down, a nifty touch that I first witnessed in Paris, at Restaurant Alain Ducasse in the Hôtel Plaza Athénée. Lee and Bigourdan opened Nota Bene late in the summer of 2008 with hopes of appealing to a broader and less stuffy audience, and it worked out for them so well that they decided to sell Splendido. And the highly accessible Nota Bene has thrived ever since. When I arrived for the game dinner at close to six o'clock in the evening on that cold November night, even the long bar was full, and the only empty seats in the dining room were at the big table reserved for the game extravaganza. Alas, I had not been invited, so I mournfully looked over the splendid collection of grand crus from Bordeaux and Burgundy breathing on the side table, and moved on to the kitchen.

There I found David Lee's faithful chef Geoff O'Connor at the pass, as usual, calling out orders, checking plates, and projecting a contagious calm from the helm even at the peak of the mad dinnertime rush. While chef Lee conceives the Nota Bene menus and oversees most lunch and dinner services, he works neither pass nor line here, and seldom has. The only exceptions are special events. Such as for those old Splendido addicts who refuse to accept that times have changed and will happily pay extra for a taste of the past in the form of a Lee-authored gastronomic tasting menu. And this happens with increased frequency in the autumn, with the concurrent onset of white truffle season and the festive run-up to Christmas.

This is not always convenient. But fortunately the only ingredient chef Lee loves working with more than truffles is game; and when a customer requests a no-holds-barred tasting menu focusing on both, Lee would not miss it for anything. He could not, anyway, because the kitchen at Nota Bene was set up to produce food of nearly bistro-basic simplicity, not tasting menus, and the line cannot handle both at the same time. So when the main line is in full swing, special menus here are produced from the back of the kitchen, largely from a six-burner hob situated across the counter from the pastry kitchen. Pulling off a lofty tasting menu in such environs requires a uniquely Lee skill set. And so that is where I found him, down the corridor past his office, beyond the shelves laden with jars of dried chicken skin, dehydrated morels, and pickled spears of white asparagus and wild ginger—all the way at the back of the kitchen, in the space shared by the adjacent patisserie and garde-manger. This would be his HQ for the evening. With only nine plates to turn out for each course (eight for the dining room, one for me), he had two chefs at his exclusive disposal—and plenty of others ready to jump if summoned. The kitchen set-up might have been less than ideal, but three chefs for nine covers is a locally unheard-of multiple-Michelin-starred-kitchen level of staffing.

When I said hello to Lee he was running his chefs through some course descriptions and putting his finishing touches in his *mise en place*. The kitchen phone rang and Lee ignored it—but then O'Connor materialized at his side. "Chef, it's Wanda. She's at the airport. She's coming here first." That would be Wanda Srdoc, more commonly know as the Truffle Lady. "She's cute, and she smells of truffles," a very successful Toronto chef had texted me, along with her phone number, when she arrived on the scene nearly a decade ago. When I hooked up with her to score shortly thereafter, I learned that Srdoc was Croatian, and has family there still, harvesting the very same indigenous white truffles that often cross the border into Italy to be sold at the Alba market as real Alba-sourced truffles at the much higher local price. Some years her truffles trump the Alba product, sometimes the two products are interchangeable, and sometimes not.

"I've got truffle from three different places already," Lee told me. "And now Wanda. I guess we'll try hers later, too."

Well, why not?

"Guys!" Lee called out to his chefs, collectively. "Gimme the first white."

The truffle Lee was handed was easily two inches in diameter, and its aroma was magnificently potent. Word came from the dining room that the game dinner guests had all arrived, so Lee put the truffle aside on a board with a slicer and got to work on his first course. To begin, he was going the classical route of truffled scrambled eggs (nice free-range eggs from Church Hill farm, in Punkeydoodles Corners, Ontario). He had not already infused the eggs with truffle, as some chefs do, packaging eggs and naked truffle together in a sealed container for a few days before cooking them. Instead, he broke his eggs into the skillet and seasoned them with salt and pepper at the outset, then whipped them vigorously, moving the pan on and off the burner constantly to moderate the heat, rather than resorting to a double boiler. As he worked a head waiter turned up at his side.

"Chef? How long for the first course? Five minutes?"

"Yes," Lee replied without looking up.

No more than thirty seconds later Bigourdan appeared.

"How long for the first course, Chef?" Bigourdan asked his partner, in his charming French accent. "Two minutes?"

"Yes," Lee replied again, without looking up.

When Bigourdan left, Lee called out for whipped cream. "And give me a spoon," he barked, to no one in particular.

No fewer than five chefs quickly materialized, each proffering a spoon for Lee. Even O'Connor had come all the way over from his station at the pass. "What do you need, Chef?"

Lee said nothing as he folded the whipped cream into his cooked eggs along with a little minced chive.

"Truffle!"

The truffle was handed over. Lee demonstrated to his two chefs how he wanted the perfectly toasted fingers of brioche arranged on each plate alongside the small mound of scrambled egg. The chef across the counter from him immediately got it backwards, forgetting that he was looking at Lee's plate upside down.

"Right-fucking-handed!" Lee said.

They got it right the second time, and when each plate was adorned with both eggs and toast, Lee shaved a dazzling amount of truffle over them.

"It's a beautiful thing," a sous-chef named Trevor muttered as he walked past.

Indeed, creamy egg and white truffle are always a heavenly pairing, whatever the time of day. And the brioche was a perfect accompaniment, the crumb within the crisp exterior very nearly as buttery and creamy as the eggs. As I ate, Lee was already plating the next dish, an intermezzo of chilled jellied wild salmon consommé with shaved truffle of a different source. Then Srdoc walked in the back door with a big Styrofoam box full of yet more truffles. She popped open the lid, and the aroma in the kitchen was nudged a level closer to being utterly overwhelming. Lee plucked one from her box and tested its aroma and texture. He appeared to be unmoved, but bought a couple anyway. Srdoc had supplied Lee with Croatian white truffles since Splendido days—and evidently he deemed the relationship to be important to preserve, even when quality varied unfavourably. So it goes with nature's goods.

Next, Lee plated a warm course of Alaskan chinook salmon, cutting it in bite-size pieces and then allowing them to be heated through—but barely—in the bath of hot fish consommé ladled overtop. The lean salmon shared space with slivered matsutake, or pine, mushrooms and a sprig of lightening cilantro. Then Lee produced a game terrine, which consisted of very lightly seared fillets of teal, pheasant, mallard, and king buck, all pressed together into the base of a terrine, with the balance of the mould filled with whole foie gras. The colours were fantastic: the bottom two-thirds of each slice was crimson, punctuated only with a stripe of pale pheasant, and topped with the unmistakable buttery caramel of cured foie gras. Naturally he then shaved truffle all over it: black ones this time, from Italy, and surprisingly pungent for the time of year (they peak at the end of January). The terrine was really more like a *pressé*, and each of its constituent game meats was so lightly cooked that they sometimes separated one from another as the terrine was cut apart. Their distinct and assertive flavours stood out enough to be readily identifiable for what they were, unmuddled, even when smeared with a little of the cured foie gras. That was a lot of flavour for a cold plate, and Lee followed it with a hot dish of lightly seared breast of teal and mallard, the unexpectedly tender crimson slices of the wild fowl draped over more pine mushrooms—braised caps this time—drizzled with a dark game bird jus and scattered with black truffle from Burgundy. Then Chef took a wise step back from all that intensity of flavour with a simple but exquisite fresh taglioni with butter and white truffles.

At this point word evidently reached the dining room that there was an imposter in the kitchen, freeloading on their meal at the source. So two of Latner's dinner guests showed up to see what was going on. Fortunately, they were friends of mine: Josh Josephson (owner of the Josephson Opticians chain) and Steve Alexander (owner of Cumbrae's, Canada's premier butcher shop). Better yet, they came bearing gifts. One, anyway: a glass of the 1990 Château Latour they had been enjoying with the pasta. Nice.

You might well think that white truffle pasta with a glass of 1990 Latour would be impossible to top, and with a half-dozen courses to go, amount to a set-up for disappointment. Not to worry. For next up, Lee produced the most exceptional wild turkey breast, which had been seared and then butter-poached— not in a saucepan, as one would do with blanched lobster, but ever so gently heated through sous-vide, in a sealed bag bulging with beurre monté. The flesh of the turkey showed a hint of pink and the thick fibre of its musculature was shockingly supple. Lee served it glazed in its emulsified poaching butter. And naturally he then shaved more white truffle all over it, and the fowl was exquisite. We moved on next to an ode to Quebec that could warm the coldest winter night: a tourtière of mixed game meats plated with the small legs of mallard duck that had been cooked to submission in a pressure cooker, then doused with wild duck jus. Beans laced with diced pork belly were served on the side.

After that Lee briefly lightened up the procession with a second consommé, this one made from his game birds and infused with cloves, cinnamon, and crushed white pepper. A cabbage roll stuffed with salted pork belly was adrift in it, along with shards of cured foie gras that he had frozen and then sliced as thin as prosciutto on an electric slicer. There were truffles, too, naturally—and the magic of the dish revolved around the echo of their nuttiness in the sprinkling of chopped toasted hazelnuts he applied to the dish for a final touch. The dish was another gem, but Lee was far from done. Next he served a slice of seared breast of wild goose with another slice of rare loin of elk, draped over a latke with a side of applesauce. Finally there was roast loin of king buck with wild blueberry sauce, and sweetly sauced braised moose, with pearl onions and baby turnips. Dessert he kept mercifully simple: apple galette with wild blueberries and vanilla ice cream.

The meal was an education. We are accustomed to eating our tender and relatively bland farm-raised ducks, venison, and elk seared rare, but more often than not their wild brethren are served over-marinated and braised, for fear of their gamy taste and stringy, lean texture. But of the eleven wild meats Lee had cooked, only a handful (mallard legs, turkey breast, tourtière, and moose) had been exposed to heat long enough to even warm them through to the centre of the cut. The resulting textures were never chewy, but as assertively variable as the flavours. As good offal does, the game had left me marvelling at the blandness of so much of the meat we eat. "There is no better chef in town with game," Josh Josephson proclaimed, when I settled in at his table in the dining room for digestifs. "None. He has been cooking it so long … "

Indeed, chef Lee's experience with game does not stop at cooking it, but extends to hunting it, too—and he is the only chef I know who has experience both with hunting fruit bats in Mauritius and shooting game birds at Sandringham. And no, he was not poaching there. Lee was born in the New Town of Stevenage, in Hertfordshire, about fifty kilometres north of London. Both his grandfathers hailed from Beijing but lived in Mauritius; David moved there when he was six, and then returned to England at age ten. But Lee continued to visit family in Mauritius each year until he quit the U.K. for Canada in 1994. Two generations of chefs preceded David in the Lee family; he grew up in a household where food was of paramount importance. Game is a staple of the English table, and venison is a favourite. They have deer in Mauritius, too. The fruit bat is more of an appetizer sort of catch.

"You see them coming down from the mountains at sunset, heading for the mango groves," Lee once explained to me. "You shoot them with a shotgun, and the dogs collect them."

Just like ducks, in other words. Except that they have to be peeled rather than feathered. You cook them as for any game bird salmis, with cinnamon, cloves, thyme, and a little sugar for seasoning. The meat is dark and sweet. Shooting at Sandringham came later. First, Lee learned to cook in the professional kitchen, starting out in small restaurants in Hertfordshire, where game was common fare. At seventeen he left for London, making the jump to the posh InterContinental Park Lane overlooking Hyde Park, where he worked at the Michelin-starred Le Soufflé under the late Peter Kromberg. Next he went abroad, to Hotel La Fleur du Lac, in Morges, on Lake Geneva, in Switzerland. In 1992 he returned to England to work for the great Swiss chef Anton Mosimann, who by then had left the Dorchester Hotel—where he ran the first hotel restaurant outside of France to earn two Michelin stars—to set up his private club in Belgravia, Mosimann's. The Swiss chef then held (and still holds) a royal warrant as caterer for the Prince of Wales. Cooking for the royals requires access to the finest game, and hunting access to Sandringham was a standard feature of its procurement.

"We'd usually go and shoot for two weeks," Lee recalls of fetching game for the royal table. "We'd stay on the grounds the whole time."

So now you know: wild deer, rabbits, and game birds may be unfit for the Canadian restaurant menu, but are more than good enough for the royal family.

On a trip to Paris in the autumn of 2004, I happened upon a wonderful butcher shop in Les Halles, which in its display case had three plump Scottish grouse, lined up in a row on their backs, with the plumage pulled back to expose their semi-putrid breasts. Obviously I felt a great need to smuggle them home.

For *Lagopus lagopus scoticus*, the red or Scotch grouse—or *la grouse*, as the French call them—is the most coveted of game birds. "While nearly all the game birds are good, and some eminently good, grouse seems to me to ... possess the fullest and at the same time the least violent flavour [and] the best consistency of flesh," George Saintsbury, celebrated author of *Notes on a Cellar-Book*, ventured in *Cookery* in 1894. "Scotch grouse [is] the best, in our opinion, of all game birds in the world," the esteemed André Simon added to the record some forty years later in his *Concise Encyclopaedia of Gastronomy*. "Nothing can beat it," Sir Anton Mosimann wrote succinctly in *The Essential Mosimann*, of serving grouse in the Grill Room at the Dorchester Hotel in London in the early eighties, when a young Marc Thuet was enlisted there as one of his young chefs.

Getting these birds from Paris to Thuet's kitchen to my plate was clearly the right thing to do. But how? My first thought was to buy a birdcage, load the dead grouse into it, check the package in at the Air Canada desk at de Gaulle, and upon landing attempt to distract the customs officials at Pearson with wild and tearful accusations about how Air Canada had killed my pets. But this plan hatched in desperation seemed a bit far-fetched—and it was far from certain that the dead birds would be released to me by customs for the proper burial I would insist on. So instead

I leaned on a local friend to have them vacuum-packed under very low pressure, and then I stuffed them into my carry-on bag. Naturally, when the baggage-scanner operator at de Gaulle saw the birds and their little up-stretched claws lined up in my case, he waved me on without even mentioning it.

The grouse grew a little more putrid on the journey home. When, late on the afternoon of my arrival, Thuet opened the package in the kitchen at The Fifth, where he was then executive chef, the stench wafted all the way across the dining room and down the corridor to the office of restaurant owner Libell Geddes. She was not at all pleased. Thuet, however, was delighted. And the grouse he made for me and my mother the following evening, with their lightly seared breasts served in a jus made from the legs, thighs, innards, and a few cloudberries, was so exquisite that Thuet immediately got to work on establishing his own far more reliable smuggling network. By the time he opened Bistro and Bakery Thuet on King Street West in 2005, I was eating grouse at his restaurant every autumn.

Over in the U.K., hunting season for Scottish grouse begins on August 12—or as they call it, "the Glorious Twelfth." So, give the birds a few weeks to hang, then arrange legal shipment to the United States, have chef Thuet drive down to the depot to inspect them and, just possibly, stuff a sackful into the spare tire cover on the back of his SUV—and come the end of September or early October, you would find me at the bar of his restaurant, eagerly poised to tuck in. Picture this: the two breasts of one of the plump little birds, each skinned and then lightly seared in a pan oiled with butter, cooked until dark brown without, crimson and barely warm within, stacked one atop the other over a hefty slab of *foie gras de canard poêlé*, which is in turn perched on a slice of brioche toasted crisp and smeared with a foie gras and pork liver mousse, heavily spiked—Alsatian-style—with Marc de Gewürztraminer. The periphery of the plate is dressed up with a judicious scattering of jackfruit brunoise, jackfruit purée, and a reduction of elderberry.

A first, small taste of the bird reminds me that Saintsbury, Simon, and Mosimann all got it exactly right. Quiet contemplation of a second forkful, meticulously assembled so as to represent a small sample of every element of taste on the plate, reveals something more: that this particular dish is classic Thuet. Very few chefs can conjure so many different flavours to come and play together on the palate in such harmony—even as each asserts itself so distinctly without getting muddled on the palate. The Thuet style also often shows a casual expertise in the preparation of game and foie gras. It involves unexpected flavours—like the jackfruit and elderberry. It also leans knowledgeably on tradition, giving it a sensible and often playful rethink (the toasted brioche is a delicate echo of the pan-dripping-drenched toast that the English traditionally serve with their roasted game birds). There is usually an inclination to be a little over the top—you may drag that once crisp brioche through your elderberry sauce if you like, but it is already infused with the juices bleeding from the grouse, the fatty runoff from the seared foie gras, as well as that of the mousse melting beneath it. If that sounds like overkill, be advised that one year's grouse à la Thuet featured grouse breast roasted with raw foie gras and an envelope of foie gras mousse *en croûte*

Roast Grouse with Braised Pears, Baby Onions, Chanterelles, and Red Wine Reduction

Chef Marc Thuet

Serves 4

4 well-hung Scottish (red) grouse
2 tsp (10 mL) olive oil
Salt and pepper
1/2 cup (125 mL) granulated sugar
1/4 cup (60 mL) vinegar
4 small pears (such as Forelle or Seckel), peeled
1/2 cup (125 mL) cold butter
1-1/2 cups (375 mL) chanterelles, trimmed and cleaned
1-1/2 cups (375 mL) pearl onions, blanched and peeled
1 cup (250 mL) red wine
1/2 cup (125 mL) game bird or duck jus
3 oz (85 g) speck, diced

Preheat oven to 350°F (180°C). Rub the grouse lightly with oil, season with salt and pepper, place in a roasting pan, and roast on the middle rack of the oven for 25 minutes. Meanwhile, fill a saucepan with enough water to cover the pears, bring to a boil over medium-high heat, add the sugar and vinegar, and stir until the sugar has completely dissolved. Reduce the heat, add the pears, and poach until soft but not falling apart—10 to 15 minutes.

Melt 2 tbsp (30 mL) butter in a cast-iron or non-stick skillet on medium-low heat. Add the pears, mushrooms, and onions, and cook, adding more butter if necessary, until the pears begin to caramelize—about 10 minutes.

Remove the grouse from the oven and set them aside to rest. Thoroughly deglaze the roasting pan with the wine, add the game or duck jus, and heat through. Strain the liquid through a fine sieve into a saucepan. Add the speck and reduce by two-thirds. Correct seasonings and whisk in 1/4 cup (60 mL) of butter, a few cubes at a time. Place the grouse on 4 serving plates with a pear and a serving of chanterelles and onions. Top with a generous serving of red wine reduction with speck.

sauced with a reduction of local wild blueberries. The last thing you need to know about "à la Thuet" is that it never means the same thing twice.

At 28 rue du Canal d'Alsace, in Thuet's hometown of Blodelsheim, you will find Hôtel Restaurant Chez Pierre, an eighty-seat restaurant of unassuming appearance that in spring and fall, anyway, is hard to miss because of the tour buses that are invariably parked outside, disgorging hungry Swiss hunters in need of such local delicacies as white asparagus and wild game killed and cooked by someone else. These days, that would be Thuet's cousin Jacques, but back when young Marc was growing up here, it was his uncle Pierre who was chef and owner. Thuet's father was a farmer, and his mother, like almost every other farmer's wife in Alsace, had an acre of the family plot to call her own, which she used to grow asparagus to sell for personal spending money. That would be white asparagus, the only kind they grow or eat here. So while Thuet's first kitchen job as a child was restaurant garbage duty— say, mopping up the spilled blood and unwanted entrails from a freshly slaughtered wild boar—in the month of May, when asparagus season starts, things were more agreeable. All he had to do was get out of bed a couple of hours earlier than the school day required so that he could peel a few hundred asparagus spears before heading off to classes, and then peel a few hundred more when he got home in the late afternoon. And while it was some years back that he first told me about this business of the asparagus farm, for some reason the recollection eluded me one spring day when I dropped in on Thuet for lunch, selected for a starter a course of white asparagus with sauce gribiche, found them to be a little overdone, and foolishly elected to say as much.

"You don't know shit about asparagus. People here who want them al dente are all idiots!" said Thuet, a large man who fills his chef's jacket in every available direction, is unshaven six days out of seven, and, according to my files both photographic and anecdotal, has removed only once the mirrored wraparound sunglasses that he sports clamped tight like a headband over his spiky blond hair—when posing for a photograph with President Bill Clinton after preparing his lunch at Frank Stronach's private Magna golf course. "When you hold it, an asparagus should look like this," he continued, first holding out his well-scarred forefinger straight and rigid, and then allowing it to droop slightly. "It should look like a cock that's just come—but it's still just a little bit interested."

At Chez Pierre, after asparagus duty at age six, Thuet graduated to plucking pheasant and partridge and skinning rabbit and hare. By the time he was twelve, his uncle began using him as cheap kitchen labour, helping out at all stations and now and then replacing chefs who missed work, like a junior tournant. His cousins Jacques and Patrick worked alongside.

Uncle Pierre—who by the by was not the first Pierre of Chez Pierre, but the third—had other passions. Twice a year, he went hunting wild boar with a gang of friends who enjoyed the sport. They were all chefs, and fine ones, too. Back when, unlike today, Michelin stars were extraordinarily hard to come by, young Marc finessed his understanding of the connection between guns and dinner in the company of hunters like Émile Jung (Au Crocodile, Strasbourg, three Michelin stars), Antoine Westermann (Restaurant Buerehiesel, Strasbourg, three Michelin stars), Pierre Gaertner (Aux Armes de France, Ammerschwihr, two Michelin stars), and the late Bernard Loiseau (La Côte d'Or, Saulieu, three Michelin stars), the brilliant chef who made the classic dish of frogs' legs, garlic, and parsley his very own—but was less than ideally suited to keeping all those hunting rifles lying around.

Young Marc, meanwhile, knew from an early age that he wanted to be a chef, and so as a teenager he enrolled at the Institut Régional de Tourisme et d'Hôtellerie, in Strasbourg. He graduated two years later with top honours and ended up on the dean's list, an achievement he celebrated on graduation day by making a heap of all the suits he had been obliged to wear at school, dousing them with lighter fluid, and setting them alight, an initiative that swiftly attracted the local fire department. "I was a little bit hammered," he concedes. His school years were marked by one other miscalculation: "I always told my friends, 'We're going to be chefs—what the fuck do you think you have to learn English for?'" Thuet followed his own advice, and this suited him fine as he completed *stage* after *stage* in the best restaurants in Alsace, landing eventually at Restaurant L'Ecureuil in Riquewihr, where chef Michel Roëlly decided his young apprentice should follow tradition and move on to hone his talents and widen his horizons abroad. Roëlly dispatched young Thuet—unconsulted, and very surprised—to London, where he had arranged a job for him with his friend and former colleague (at the Palace Hotel in St. Moritz) Anton Mosimann, at the Dorchester Hotel.

Thuet arrived for duty, age nineteen, with barely a word of English at his disposal, but he learned fast, seizing first upon the word people in the kitchen appeared to use most and making it a signature catch-all. "I was in London for two years before I finally learned what 'fucking' meant," he concedes now. But then, he was busy learning a lot of other things: Mosimann was then in the process of revolutionizing not just the culinary vision of the grand old Dorchester but also that of the country at large. In the Dorchester's Grill Room, the tired staples of traditional British cookery—from roast grouse with drippings on toast to steak and kidney pie and bread-and-butter pudding—were being lightened and reinvented with a finesse from which they had long been estranged. At the Terrace, Mosimann was developing his concept of cuisine naturelle, a style of cooking that incorporated the healthful lessons of nouvelle cuisine in a new culinary philosophy that was far more substantive and emphasized seasonality and the purest, unadulterated flavours. And he ensured its popularity by fielding his new ideas in the framework of what was then the entirely new concept of *menu surprise*, wherein diners sat down trustingly to a six-course meal without any idea of what was to come.

"I had worked in three-stars all over Alsace. I never saw cooking like that," Thuet reflected of the cooking at the Terrace in those early days, put out by Mosimann and his chef Ralph Bürgin, who had previously worked with the legendary Eckart Witzigmann at his three-starred Aubergine in Munich. "Chefs like Hans-Peter Wodarz and Roger Vergé came from all over Europe to see what they were doing. I thought if Mosimann didn't get three stars, I wouldn't believe it."

Thuet was first stationed in the kitchen at the Grill Room because he was deemed too young to cook for the Terrace. But he offered to do it for free, and finally one day when the poissonier called in sick on the tournant's day off, Thuet got his chance— and thereafter the Terrace was where he stayed, moving to saucier and finally becoming an unofficial chef tournant. The restaurant never received its anticipated three stars, but it did become the first hotel restaurant outside France to ever be awarded two of them. Meanwhile, after two years in London, Thuet was growing restless and seeking a post in the United States. Mosimann intervened and instead secured him a job in Canada, a stepping stone, with his mentor, the great Swiss chef Albert Schnell, who had been executive chef at the Queen Elizabeth Hotel in Montreal when Mosimann, drawn by the promise of Expo 67, signed up there as sous-chef in 1966. Fifteen years later, Schnell was at the Harbour Castle Hilton in Toronto. Thuet arrived for work in early 1984, beginning as chef de partie. Within a week his colleagues had a new nickname for him: they called him Fucking.

After a year at the Hilton, Thuet moved on to the Windsor Arms Hotel, and from there, in 1989, to Centro Grill & Wine Bar on Yonge Street, where in 1993 he became executive chef. The next year, shopping around for a new chef, he called his old mentor Anton Mosimann in London for help. Mosimann sent Thuet a young chef named David Lee. But within a couple of years, tensions between Thuet and his partners had the whole Centro ownership structure under severe strain.

One Sunday in 2001, I went to visit Thuet at his farmhouse near Pefferlaw, an hour from Toronto on Lake Simcoe. He had been toying for some time with the idea of selling his Centro stake and establishing a restaurant at the farm, so he had invited me out with my family for brunch and to have a look at the place. When we pulled up around noon, his truck was nowhere to be seen, and when I knocked on the door, it was his girlfriend and future wife, Biana, who answered.

"Marc's next door. He had to kill a bear," she explained matter-of-factly.

Indeed, as it turned out, his neighbour was an apiarist, and for some weeks, a local bear had been availing himself liberally of the honey supply. The neighbour appealed to Thuet for help, and that night when he arrived home from work, Chef grabbed a hunting rifle, drove into his neighbour's driveway, focused his headlights on the apiary, and with his gun hanging out the window, he watched and waited, waited some more, and dozed off. Sometime later, a little rustling woke him up and he let off a quick shot, but the bear stumbled off into the darkness. Never follow an injured bear into the woods at night, the old Alsatian saying goes, so Thuet rolled up the window and went back to sleep. When he awoke, he found that the bear had only made it a few feet. And now, there it was on its side, with Thuet's young son Jules giving it a prod with his foot, which was causing blood to spurt from the wound. Thuet began hammering its rear paws onto a two-by-four so he could hoist it over a tree branch to dress it. At which point my daughter, Simone, just three at the time, asked me why Thuet had killed the animal.

"He was a bad bear," I explained. "He was stealing honey."

Then, remembering that she was big into Winnie-the-Pooh, who had very similar habits, I dispatched her, her brother, Max, and their mother back to Thuet's house to wait. And just in time, for they cleared the shielding hedge just as the bear's entrails tumbled vigorously out of the carcass and onto the ground. Thuet was shoulder-deep in the thing when I asked his seven-year-old daughter, Robbie, who was standing and watching right in front of me, if she wanted to go back to the house, too. She looked, eyes open wide, wrinkled her nose, and giggled a little.

"This is the grossest thing I've seen Daddy do since that time he cut the head off that pig and it ran off into the road and he couldn't find it!"

The bear yielded some excellent tenderloin, and a year or two later, its hind legs—like those of so many of Thuet's pigs before it, raised on Centro slop—matured into superior prosciutto. And this was just one in a long sequence of local wild game meats he has prepared for me and a select few over the years. I will never forget his sensational civet of deer ("Bambi walked in front of the wrong house," he said at the time), or the terrines with noisettes of wild Arctic hare, and breast of wild pheasant and woodcock. Alas, all of it forbidden on his restaurant menus, unless sold by stealth. Once, I had the misfortune of strolling into his office at Bistro and Bakery Thuet just as he slammed down the phone with Canada Customs, which had just seized a shipment of his Scottish grouse.

"A Sikh can wear a turban in the fucking RCMP but a fucking French chef can't cook grouse?" he bellowed at me. "It's a fucking outrage!"

It is. And it is also an outrage that Canadian chefs cannot use their restaurants to showcase our own wild grouse, turkeys, deer, hare, rabbit, and every other game animal across the land. For game is one of our great resources, and in keeping it out of the hands of real chefs who know what to do with it, and leaving it entirely to home cooks, who do not, we have defaulted on developing what might have become the cornerstone of our national cuisine. So even today, if you really want to eat great Canadian game, as our own chefs generally lack experience with it, you do best to import for the occasion a great European-trained chef, like David Lee or Marc Thuet. This situation strikes me as absurd and rather sad.

～ 6 ～

HAUTE CUISINE
IN QUEBEC

While in Quebec City in 2008 partaking of its four-hundredth anniversary celebrations, I learned that the precocious locavore Samuel de Champlain had jumped the gun some on Niagara and the Okanagan, and way back in 1608 had a go at starting a vineyard on the outskirts of his new settlement. Needless to say, those vines of *Vitis vinifera* that he had brought along from France for the purpose did not survive their first New World winter. But of course that was not the worst of it, and accounts of that particular misadventure got lost in the rest of the horror.

Fortunately, the little town where we got started has come along some in the interim. A research trip to the birthplace of Canadian cuisine like the one I took that year can now be comfortably managed from the highly salubrious locale of the Auberge Saint-Antoine, a lovely Relais & Châteaux in Old Quebec, situated on the riverbank right across the street from the Musée de la Civilisation. The auberge in its present form opened in November 2003, and it is unique. In a time of cookie-cutter boutique hotels, where the lobby bar at, say, the Morrison in Dublin looks and feels exactly like that at the Clift in San Francisco or the Paramount in New York, this one is unmistakably Quebec. It is ultra-modern but simultaneously looks to the local past, and shines a light on it, too. Much of its decor was sourced from the archaeological excavation that preceded the laying of its foundation here on what a few centuries back were the city docks. So there is a rare French cannon sitting behind glass in the bar, and the backlit display boxes in the lobby feature seventeenth-century pipes, pottery, and the craziest-looking giant hand-hammered fish hooks you have ever seen. One shudders to think about what they reeled in with them; I've caught four-hundred-pound marlin on hooks half the size.

The hotel's restaurant, Panache, is housed in a two-hundred-year-old waterside warehouse, and some of the old pulleys that the British used to unload their ships are still mounted in the ceiling, where they are integrated into the design. As with the rest of the hotel, the idea of the restaurant is to be contemporary but with one foot firmly planted in the past. So the cooking is modern but many of the culinary ideas share conspicuous lineage with the food of our early settlers. Pop by for a bite nowadays and you will find on the menu things like spit-roasted duck glazed with maple syrup, or roast *gigot* (leg) of venison—albeit perfectly legal farmed venison, from a farm in Quebec's Appalachians—with a classic cloudberry sauce. François Blais, the young Quebec chef who opened the restaurant in 2004, has since moved on to open his own place, Bistro B, in Montcalm, a few blocks from the Plains of Abraham. When he was at Panache in 2008 and charged with creating a special menu to commemorate the four-hundredth anniversary of his hometown, he started with predictable contemporary classics like oysters, and a *torchon* of foie gras with cranberry chutney, and then moved right into *perdrix* (partridge) with braised cabbage with juniper berries, and a main course of *bouilli de cerf de Boileau façon Panache*—which is to say, a sort of pot-au-feu of venison (raised at a well-known farm in the Outaouais).

"There were partridge all through the woods here in 1608," Blais affirmed to *L'actualité* at the time, in explanation of his choices. "We've been eating deer here for four hundred years."

He's right—but then, Henry VIII liked his venison too, and long before him, so did Vercingetorix, king of the Gauls. All our ancestors did. And such is usually the case with just about everything we consider Canadian foods and the way we choose to eat them. Even those comically all-Canadian menus we put on for visiting dignitaries at Rideau Hall invariably focus on "our" indigenous ingredients that you can easily source elsewhere. The Americans make perfectly good maple syrup, caribou is consumed in every nation that touches the Arctic Circle (they just prefer to call it reindeer), those spot prawns Vancouver chefs like to pretend they discovered were featured on Jeremiah Tower's menus at Stars in San Francisco two decades ago, and sadly, while you may consider Nova Scotia lobster to be the best in the world, some years ago the late great Spanish chef Santi Santamaria assured me that if a Michelin inspector ever caught him using one in place of blue lobster from the North Atlantic at his three-Michelin-star restaurant Can Fabes, near Barcelona, *"Mon troisième macaron—bye-bye."*

All this contributes to the fact that Canadian cuisine can be difficult to define. But the job is generally easier in the province of Quebec than in the rest of Canada, for the customary combined reasons of linguistic insulation from the cultural behemoth to the south, and their considerable head start. All the same, Quebec City itself is a small town with an economy focused on tourism and government. Even individually, those qualities generally translate into bad restaurants; combine all three and bad, overpriced food is all but guaranteed. It is easy, for example, to make the innocent mistake of strolling out of the front doors of the glorious Château Frontenac and right there, on Rue Saint-Louis, being tempted by the sight of the lovely white stuccoed facade of a little house built by one François Jacquet in 1675, which nearly three hundred years later was converted into a restaurant called Aux Anciens Canadiens—as it remains today. It looks to be a pleasant spot, neither pretentious nor excessively tourist-baiting, and what's more, when I happened upon it there was a lineup snaking out the front door all the way to the sidewalk.

My wife, Lisa, and I unsuspectingly joined the queue. Next thing I knew I was contemplating a plate of what, for three and a half glorious centuries before poutine, was incontestably the most famous of Quebec culinary creations: not pea soup or *oreilles de crisse*, but tourtière. Sizing up this particular slab of compacted grey ground meats, the damp, leaden pastry encircling it, and the moat of gluey brown sauce serving as its line of outer defence, all that I could think to myself in my distressed hunger was, "In all of culinary history, has one region of a nation ever squandered a three-hundred-year head start enjoyed over the rest of the country quite so catastrophically as this?"

I knew better—but not enough to have made a decent restaurant choice. Still, at least I was getting out there. Which is to say that this once I was doing better than my father, who particularly enjoyed telling a story about having once written a travel piece about Quebec City for *The New York Times* without having ever left the bed in his suite at the Château Laurier, where he had been felled by a bad cold. The 2008 trip was my first visit to Quebec City since that inevitable high school excursion to see those fateful plains, and later that day, our first dinner, at a highly recommended restaurant in Saint-Roch, had also proved a bust. But all the same, around noon the next day, Lisa and I strolled out of the Saint-Antoine in good spirits, charged by the warm glow of the nearing springtime sun and the cobblestone aesthetics of the splendid old Basse-Ville. We had a booking at Restaurant Initiale, less than a block along Rue Saint-Pierre in the lovely 1866 Union Bank of Lower Canada building.

The facade is splendid, and my spirits and culinary expectations rose as I quickly looked over the menu posted on the heavy wooden door. Inside, part-owner and front-of-house manager Rolande Leclerc welcomed us warmly. Then she led us unbidden directly to the ideal romantically secluded table for two, which is tucked into a corner at the front of the room, largely hidden by the curved screen that separates dining room from entrance hall. The cocktails were mixed perfectly. The menu offered a surplus of enticing choice, and when after some exhaustive consideration

I finally came up with a compromise that mixed elements from the table d'hôte with others from la carte, Leclerc dismissed the potential complication with gracious flexibility. And then I was promptly served my first course: *morilles et asperges au vin jaune, homard saisi, et crème de petits pois.*

Morels sprout in Quebec a good three weeks after they first appear in B.C., and the local edition tends to be smaller, too. But they are very much worth waiting for; they have a darker cap and are generally acknowledged to be slightly superior in flavour and texture. The three or four on my plate had, according to French tradition, been sautéed in butter in a hot pan that was next deglazed with fortified wine, in this case vin jaune. There was a judicious drizzle of that, too, on my small handful of perfectly poached local white and green asparagus. The lobster was represented by a single plump claw. It had first been parboiled so as to encourage it to part ways with its shell, just as you would do if you were going to butter-poach it. But for the next step the de-cloaked lobster had been quickly fried in hot butter, which is a far trickier proposition that requires much more precision of timing than merely steeping the stuff in a bath of beurre monté at 180°F for five or six minutes. In this approach, if the pan is too hot, or if the lobster is left in it a moment too long, its flesh will be vulcanized. Chef, though, had done it precisely right. Its colour, enhanced by a light sprinkle of paprika and curry powder, ran from vivid orange to red. The claw had a hint of lightly crisped caramelization around its periphery, but within, the meat was soft, sweet, and supple. The small pool of puréed spring peas beneath added one more lovely taste of spring to the standard-bearers of asparagus and morels, and the drizzle of translucent yellow sauce of nutty vin jaune, that distinctive late-harvest white wine from the French Jura, exquisitely bridged the beautifully chosen array of delicate flavours and pretty colours.

One of my favourite and best-thumbed cookbooks is called *Keep it Simple*, by Alastair Little, an English chef of considerable influence back in the eighties when he opened an eponymous restaurant on Frith Street, in Soho, London. The virtue of simplicity is a constant refrain of the best chefs, from Marco Pierre White and Paul Bocuse to, believe it or not, even that maestro of convoluted complexity, Ferran Adrià. And to me that springtime dish of chef Yvan Lebrun's at Restaurant Initiale encapsulated perfectly what those others were getting at—for they are not talking about simplicity of technique but of conceptualization. The complexity of the cooking method is irrelevant as long as it is correctly executed and undertaken for the good of the dish—as opposed to distracting from it, by drawing attention to the chef. In a great dish, flavours should be distinct, harmonious, and never cluttered. Lebrun's lobster—as Peter Shaffer's *Amadeus* so nicely put it—had exactly the right amount of notes: nothing extra, nothing missed. And there was more to like about the Lebrun philosophy as it was expressed on that plate: here was a chef who was striving to enhance natural flavours, not to meddle with them or disguise them, and while he was clearly committed to using local ingredients of quality, he was sensibly not in the camp of the new doctrinaire breed of locavore. A 100-miler would have swapped that *vin jaune* for something produced in Quebec (like, say, a ghastly sweet ice cider, or failing that, at least some vintage from nearby Niagara). But then the dish would not have turned out as well, and as it was, it was perfect. And it was just a first course in a prix fixe lunch.

So my wife and I went back, again and again, visiting Quebec City for the express purpose of dining at Initiale. One midsummer lunch began with a delicate fillet of flaky milk-poached Saint-Pierre (John Dory) served in a little of its buttery poaching liquid with young fava beans and spinach. Next, a small sealed pot arrived on a plate; lifting its lid unleashed an arrestingly aromatic gust of steam scented with spruce and sweet garlic, and when it cleared, I found a gently baked breast of squab resting there on a bed of puréed young garlic, surrounded by a creamy sauce spiked with ground squab leg—and a tiny sprig of spruce. Then I was served a small, mildly chewy *macreuse* (or flatiron) steak plated with delicate French green beans, a purée of *blette* (Swiss chard), and a sauté of no fewer than eight different local wild mushrooms—an arrangement that, as Leclerc explained, the resolutely unpretentious chef Lebrun called "'full' *champignons*." Finally we were delivered a crispy-edged, soft-centred orange-maple biscuit with sliced peach and then a chocolate dome, firm without, moist within, spiked with cassis and almonds, and resting on a pool of apricot compote. On another occasion, a wintry meal that began with a large seared scallop sliced crosswise and resting along with a small morsel of cod in a pool of frothed, cream-spiked beurre blanc dressed with crisp-fried dill featured a showstopper: *crosnes et feuilles de Bruxelles au beurre d'arroche, royale d'oursins, et oursins de la Colombie-Britannique, thon* Big Eye. Here we had a scattering of braised Chinese artichokes, a tataki of bigeye tuna, a rectangle of sea urchin custard, and a good drizzle of orache-sweetened butter all playing counterpoint to the principal act of lobes of B.C.-sourced sea urchin cradled in blanched leaves of Brussels sprouts, a juxtaposition of the exotic and the banal that yielded such a startlingly symbiotic combination of flavours that I could have ended the meal absolutely satisfied then and there—but fortunately I did not have to.

On the northern coast of Brittany just west of the Norman border one finds a picturesque fishing village named Cancale, which, since its founding in the mid-sixth century, has managed to build up a population that now numbers just a tick over five thousand people. But if the Cancalaises themselves have proved to be reluctant breeders, the oysters that also take their name from the surrounding Baie de Cancale are quite the opposite: the 7.2 square kilometres of oyster beds that flank the town are generally good for an annual yield of some 25,000 tonnes. And these eponymous oysters—Cancales—have been of the most impeccable quality for as long as anyone can remember. A couple of millennia ago, when the local breed was flat—as in Belon, or *Ostrea edulis*, such as we now enjoy from nearby Locmariaquer—the Romans prized Cancales above any other. The Sun King, Louis XIV, agreed, and insisted on their regular presence on his breakfast table at Versailles.

Today the quality remains exceptional even though the breed has changed (an outbreak of gill disease combined with an accidental influx of *Crassostrea angulata* all but dispatched

Saffron Puff Pastry with Sea Urchin, Chinese Artichokes, and Brussels Sprouts à la soubise

Chef Yvan Lebrun

Serves 8

For the soubise
1 white onion, sliced
2 cloves garlic, crushed
1 tbsp (15 mL) butter
1 tbsp (15 mL) olive oil
1 cup (250 mL) white chicken stock
1/4 cup (60 mL) white rice
1/3 cup (75 mL) 35% cream
Salt and pepper

For the saffron pastry
1/3 cup (75 mL) 35% cream
5 threads of saffron
1/2 lb (225 g) puff pastry
1 egg yolk

For finishing
1 cup (250 mL) Chinese artichokes (crosnes), blanched and peeled
1 tbsp (15 mL) butter
16 dark green Brussels sprout leaves, blanched
16 lobes of sea urchin

For the soubise, sweat the onion and garlic in the butter and olive oil. Add the stock and rice. Simmer gently for 45 minutes. Pass through a ricer into a clean pot, fold in the cream, and season with salt and pepper. Set aside.

For the saffron pastry, preheat oven to 350°F (180°C). Heat the cream, then add the saffron and simmer gently, stirring frequently, until the cream acquires a dark saffron colour—about 5 minutes. Chill over ice or in the refrigerator. On a floured work surface roll out the pastry to a thickness of 1/8 inch (3 mm), and then cut it into 8 portions. Transfer to a baking sheet lined with parchment paper. Whisk the egg yolk into the saffron-infused cream, brush the pastry with the mixture, and bake until crisp and golden—15 to 20 minutes.

To finish, briefly sauté the artichokes in butter until they are bronzed and crisp—2 to 3 minutes. Reheat the soubise. Fold the artichokes into the soubise and spoon the mixture onto 8 warmed plates. To each portion add a pair of Brussels sprout leaves, nestle the lobes of sea urchin within, and finally place the pastry alongside.

Variation: Add a small portion of tuna tataki encrusted with Maldon sea salt and crushed black Sarawak pepper.

the Belon from local waters in the early twenties, and in the seventies the Portuguese oysters also succumbed to disease and were replaced by hardier *Crassostrea gigas* sourced from B.C.). To this day, if you find a dish on a French menu anywhere described as being prepared *à la cancalaise*, you can be assured that the fish or seafood listed there will be stuffed or at least garnished with poached oysters sourced from this very bay. Yvan Lebrun, too, was born in Cancale, where his grandparents had worked the earth and sold the local catch. His father also made his life on the open seas. And while Lebrun did not grow up wanting for anything, his youth was hardly characterized by luxury, either: he was only thirteen when the time came to leave school and enter the workforce himself. For that he abandoned Cancale and headed just up the coast to Saint Malo, where he found a job in the kitchen of a modest inn named La Métairie de Beauregard. "I did not choose the line of work," Lebrun concedes. "It was a combination of necessity and the people my parents knew."

But Lebrun was lucky. He liked the work and he liked his boss. The restaurant at La Métairie had sixty seats spread through two dining rooms and it was busy. *Chef-patron* Jacques Gonthier was a veteran of three great Parisian restaurants, each of them Michelin-starred then as they remain today: Restaurant Lasserre, Restaurant Laurent, and Restaurant Ledoyen. "He was a very talented chef, but I learned from him as much about life as I did about work. He became like a second father to me." Gonthier mentored Lebrun for more than four years. "I did everything. I washed dishes, I grated carrots, I made staff meals … " And he also learned an array of highly advanced culinary skills from an experienced chef whose culinary philosophy was completely *d'accord* with that of the majority of the best French chefs of the mid-seventies. Simply put, Gonthier worried that the new thinking of *la nouvelle cuisine* was responsible for as much harm as good. He believed in the new cooking's focus on unadulterated, natural flavours, lighter *cuisson*, healthier sauces, and the enhancement of their flavour by reduction instead of the addition of butter and flour. But he stopped shy of undercooking his fish or slapping together counterintuitive shotgun marriages of flavour conceptualized to capture the attention of the diner's eye more than his palate. "It was a very good school for me," Lebrun said. And he was a very good apprentice. "I liked the discipline, the hard work—I could have been okay in the army."

All the same, after Lebrun enlisted at nineteen to fulfill his compulsory military service, he returned to Saint Malo each weekend when he was off duty in order to take up his knives and wooden spoons once more in the kitchen at La Métairie. And two years later, when his service was complete, Lebrun promptly set off on what he likes to refer to as "*le tour.*" For the time had come to broaden horizons and learn those things that his mentor could not teach him. Lebrun restricted himself to France, starting out in the region of Languedoc-Roussillon, at Cap d'Agde on the Mediterranean coast, where he took a job at La Tamarissière. Next he moved to Chez Planes, in the Pyrenees, and on it went. "My father was a seafarer, a sailor—we moved a lot. I was used to it." Lebrun was acquiring fresh experience and new skills at some of the best kitchens in 1980s France, running the gamut of French cuisine from *traditionelle* to *nouvelle* at a series of restaurants so eminent that not one had scored below 17 (out of a theoretically possible 20) in *Le Guide Gault-Millau.* His final stop in a French kitchen had him back in the Saint Malo area, at Hôtel Le d'Avaugour in the neighbouring village of Dinan.

There, one evening in 1986, Lebrun unwittingly cooked a meal for a Frenchman named Jean Soulard, visiting from his adopted home of Quebec City, where he was executive chef at the Hilton Hotel. This was still the era when North American hotel kitchens were largely run by chauvinistic European chefs who preferred to hire European staff with the right European training, and Soulard was following convention, travelling through France with a view to harvesting new staff. Lebrun was offered a job and he accepted.

"*Je ne comprenais pas,*" Lebrun said, breaking into a smile, thinking back to that fateful decision made with such little insight into where he was headed and what it would mean.

Quebec City, winter, and the culture of the Hilton unsurprisingly amounted to a collective shock. For one thing, Lebrun had never before encountered a North American hotel waiter—not to mention the unionized edition ("*C'est effrayant!* You love your work but you have to work with *them* ... "). And of course the tourist-and-convention-driven Hilton menu was not the sort of thing he was accustomed to cooking. But there were bright moments, too. On the culinary side, after his initial appointment to serve as sous-chef under Soulard, Lebrun was swiftly promoted to a position better suited to his skill set: he was appointed banquet chef, responsible only for gastronomic dinners for groups that usually numbered between fourteen and twenty and never surpassed forty. The guests were customarily European and arrived with correspondingly sophisticated culinary expectations, and Lebrun was encouraged to meet or surpass them without referencing any hotel menus—just his own instincts. "Small VIP meals. I could do what I wanted." A lovely gig, no doubt, especially when paired with the good pay and job security that came with working for a huge and highly successful hotel chain.

And there was something else. Some*one*, actually: the maître d'hotel at the main Hilton restaurant, Le Croquembouche, was the delightful Rolande Leclerc. Four years later, partners in life, they quit the Hilton together and became partners in business, too, opening a place of their own called Le Restaurant Initiale. The original 1990 incarnation was situated on Avenue Maguire in Sillery, a quiet and prosperous outlying community overlooking the St. Lawrence from a hillside perch just west of the old walled city. "Having our own restaurant allowed me to express myself completely, to establish my real culinary identity, a way of cooking that was just like me." The process since has been one of fine-tuning. In 1998, after a long search, they purchased their dream location in the lower old town, an old bank building situated one short block from the riverfront. They have since renovated three times. "The cooking and the room must match. You evolve."

The local evolution must now be very near its zenith. Lebrun's cuisine is impeccable; it is elegant, sophisticated, inventive, and highly refined without ever veering into pretentious excess. The service reflects precisely the same qualities (well, except for the inventiveness bit), and the premises themselves make an ideal home for it all. The tall ceilings and windows of the grand old bank lobby are stunning, as are its newly acquired shades of tan, beige, and chocolate brown, the curved screens, and other elegant furnishings. The white linen–draped tables are set with lovely monogrammed plates made by Bernardaud in France and stencilled by a graphics designer in Sherbrooke, Quebec (I know because one hangs on my office wall, alongside my father's old luncheon plate from Schwartz's deli). Add up the parts and you have a restaurant that was not merely well reviewed but also, since 2006, a full-fledged member of that lofty restaurant club, Les Grands Chefs Relais & Châteaux (there are only three in the province—and four in the country at large). And in 2011, they were given Five-Diamond status by the CAA.

Lebrun himself, a proud member of the international gastronomic order of the Chaîne des Rôtisseurs, is an engaging but shy man, jovial, but uncomfortable in the spotlight, and he evidently prefers cooking to talking about how well he does it. But he makes an exception now and then, and so one afternoon he joined me for a glass of wine in his lounge at Initiale to talk a little about his philosophy of cooking. "It comes from here," he says, tapping his right temple lightly, eyes twinkling mischievously. "I really don't go out and see what others are doing for inspiration." The guiding rule of his culinary philosophy is that ingredients should taste of what they are and never be turned into something else; in keeping with that, he professes admiration for the chefs Thomas Keller and Pierre Gagnaire. As to how his cooking has changed since he arrived in Quebec in 1986, he attributes much of the evolution to the concurrent breakthrough in quality of locally produced ingredients. "*En '86, il n'y avait rien,*" he said of how dire things were when he arrived. Back then everything was imported. Even the foie gras had to be brought in from France or Hungary. "Now we have everything," he said, and broke into an easy, contented smile.

If Quebec now has everything, there is very likely one man—one chef—who is more to thank than any other: Quebec City–born Normand Laprise. And I happened to be in Quebec City in September 2008 when, under the aegis of the Québec Gourmande festival, Laprise brought his singular style of cooking back home, to be showcased for a $400-a-plate dinner at Initiale. When I got there mid-afternoon, I found Lebrun at the back of his kitchen, working with two of his staff on canapés featuring some ripe red tomatoes no larger than green peas. At another counter, two members of Laprise's ten-strong Toqué! brigade were poring over tiny wild Quebec blueberries, checking for quality and grit, while alongside, another was inspecting some locally grown grapes. Others were gathered around the stove at the centre of the kitchen, tasting sauces, checking their *mise en place*. And directing it all was frenetic Toqué! chef de cuisine Charles-Antoine Crête, one eye on the purposeful commotion unfolding around him, the other on a tray of fresh seaweed—some six types in all, harvested the day before from the St. Lawrence estuary at Kamouraska, where Laprise spent a good portion of his youth on a farm.

"We dry it and then use it in winter," Crête explained, and then holding up a particularly broad and ruddy leaf, added, "This one—*c'est comme un konbu Québécois*"—konbu being the Japanese seaweed that when steeped in water with flakes of dried bonito gives rise to the ubiquitous dashi broth.

For a chef, the business of putting on a multi-course tasting menu off-site comes with innumerable complications. One of them is that the staff at the host restaurant has no familiarity with what they are helping to assemble in the kitchen or serving in the dining room. So with a view to obviating this, Laprise wanted to walk them all through his dishes right before service. He gave the word to his chef, and Crête in turn summoned *his* chefs (*"Amène tout le monde—et bam!"* was his call to action). Laprise began the presentation to the gathered chefs with his amuse-gueule: a spoonful of vibrantly coloured flower petals, fully seasoned, tossed and chased with a shot glass of diluted yuzu juice. Laprise took a plate out to the dining room to show it to the Initiale waiters poised to serve his food for the first time, and explained it to them. And on it went—not in order, but in haphazard progress through the menu determined by a convenience dictated by *mise en place* and preparation time. Two tiny princess scallops were shucked and cleaned and returned raw to their shell, sprinkled with olive oil, floated in the juice of strawberries and red bell peppers, and topped with a foam cast from the lightly bitter, dried, and powdered blossom of the sumac tree. Then another fish course that neatly summed up the Laprise style: take one quarter-inch slice of fillet of salmon back, rendered firm and dense from its salty cure, and sandwich it with thick smoked cream between two perfectly flat potato chips sliced so thin as to be translucent.

"It tastes like smoked salmon but it's not smoked salmon," Crête explained. "It's fake smoked salmon. *C'est un* joke."

Next it was time for *foie gras chaud "fraîchement Toqué!,"* a thick slice scored and seared and served up with the pear water, jellied honey, ground cherries, and turnips. Then he did contre-filet of Angus beef (sourced from his new supplier, Steve Alexander's Cumbrae's Meats in Toronto) with roasted garlic, chanterelles, elderberries, and sauce bordelaise. Sea urchins, which only the day before had been minding their own business in the St. Lawrence off Kamouraska, were blended into cream and then returned to their formerly cozy spiny shells. A cheese called Monarque, from La Fromagerie Hamel in Saint-Rémi-de-Tingwick, was sliced as thin as a sheet of paper and draped warm over fresh Quebec berries lightly anointed with argan oil. For dessert a small Mason jar was filled with a layered array of Lac Saint-Jean blueberries, white chocolate mousse, crunchy dacquoise, blueberry sorbet, and a judicious sprinkling of tarragon oil.

"That's it," said Laprise to the waiters gathered around him and his plates in the dining room. "*C'est un bon menu.* We've got good flavours. We end summer on a good note—nice ripe flavours."

Quite so: that spoonful of seasoned flowers chased with yuzu tasted like a mouthful of summer in full glory. The firm cured salmon easily fulfilled the mission of trickery for which it was conceived. The scallops, consumed in a single slurp from the shell, were sweetly refreshing, and every last ingredient in the mix announced itself distinctly and assertively. Beneath its foamy surface, the frothed cream of sea urchin contained an unadulterated lobe, a little crunch of celery, a hint of shallot, and a faint and lightening burst of cilantro. The foie gras was exquisite. The heavily marbled beef was enticingly succulent and deeply flavoured, complemented handsomely by its topping of mildly smoky elderberries, the caramelized chanterelles, sweet roasted garlic, rosehip, and sauce bordelaise. The mild cheese draped over berries made a perfect bridge to a dessert that nicely encapsulated Laprise's simultaneous preoccupations with varied and contrasting textures, bright flavours, and a determined lack of pretense.

The wonderful American food writer Alan Richman once wrote in *GQ* magazine that "Laprise is the rarest of all chefs, an apparently out-of-control improviser with absolute command over his food and his impulses." That command is rooted in the customary long and dutiful training that began with two years of hostelry school in Charlesbourg, Quebec, followed by work and internships at all the expected long-established restaurants of Quebec City such as Café de la Paix and Le Marie-Clarisse. His progress was punctuated by jaunts abroad to France, where he served a series of apprenticeships that began in Lyons (Brasserie

Le Nord) and took him through Wettolsheim (in Alsace), Reims, and Dijon (Hôtel de la Cloche, under Jean-Pierre Billoux). The French experience acclimatized Laprise to superior artisan-sourced ingredients—and it was that as much as the techniques he acquired that set him on his particular culinary course. For when Laprise finally returned to Quebec to take a job as executive sous-chef at Le Lutétia, in Montreal's rococo Hôtel de la Montagne, and then followed that with his first gig as executive chef at Citrus, he was struck above all else by the poor quality of the ingredients in what was supposedly a destination dining city. The disparity with the ingredients he had known in France was simply too much, and his career since has in large part been defined by attempts to change that. His ability to improvise with his ingredients is a reflection of his success in the mission (ordinary ingredients and spontaneity are not such a good mix).

No other chef-proprietor in the country has worked quite as hard with as many local suppliers as has Laprise. Most of the best and most familiar Quebec products starred on his menus before anyone else's. Laprise popularized pré-salé lamb from Île Verte in the St. Lawrence, where conditions on the salt marsh replicate those that give rise to the celebrated salt marsh lamb of Normandy and Brittany. (Alas, he made it far more popular than the tiny supply can accommodate, and now the vast bulk of lamb bearing that label is no such thing. Although I have seen Quebec pré-salé on innumerable Toronto menus over the years, it is in fact regular Quebec lamb they are selling. "This is a *gros problem*," Laprise acknowledges.) His special relationship with the fishermen of Îles de la Madeleine began in 2000, when he helped establish a supply route for their razor clams to be sold at the fabulous Montreal fish market La Mer. Now he serves as the official product ambassador for everything they catch, from lobster to snow crab. In the mid-nineties, Pierre-André Daigneault's baby greens and tiny vegetables—from winter spinach to heritage carrots—acquired such a reputation through the way Laprise prepared them at Toqué! that Rob Feenie started shipping his produce by air-freight to Vancouver for use at Lumière. And working with forager François Brouillard, whom he met by chance at Montreal's Jean-Talon Market before opening Toqué!, Laprise has helped to reassert the once important culinary profile of wild Quebec herbs and plants such as glasswort, wild ginger, winter cress, elderberry, live-forever, milkweed, daylily buds, sea purslane, and sea sandwort.

Then there are the myriad products that Laprise has helped to develop. Toqué! was the first restaurant—in 1994—to serve venison raised on Denis Ferrer's farm in the Outaouais, which nowadays is ubiquitous on good menus province-wide, under the name *cerf de Boileau.*

"When Denis first came by to see me, he brought me a loin to try," Laprise recalled, relaxing over a mid-afternoon coffee at Toqué! "*C'était dur*—it was hard!" Laprise rapped his knuckles on the table for effect. "It was Thursday or Friday. I said, 'When did you kill this?' He said, 'Wednesday.' I explained that this was not how it works."

Lessons in dry-aging aside, Laprise's farming background has equipped him to work on bespoke projects with those farmers who want to supply him. For example, St-Canut cream-fed pork, which is today on tables across the United States from Thomas Keller's French Laundry to Daniel Boulud's db Bistro Moderne, Craft, and Le Cirque in New York—was born of a meeting at Toqué! in 2004.

"Normand Laprise asked me, 'How can we raise a pig that tastes like suckling pig but is bigger?' So I went back to the farm and did some homework," farmer Carl Rousseau explained to me. What he and his business partner Alexandre Aubin discovered was that while a suckling pig is congenitally programmed to refuse its mother's milk and turn to solid food at the age of eight weeks, you can trick them into staying on a dairy diet longer if you heat the milk or cream to a temperature of—well, that's a secret. But feed your little piggies that warm milk every two hours for another eight weeks and you get what Laprise ordered: a suckling pig that is bigger and fatter and juicier. And, of course, since you are what you eat, its fat will taste just like butter.

"Everybody talks about cuisine de terroir, but mine is really a cuisine de produits," Laprise said. "The principle is that you know all your suppliers. You have a relationship with everyone, and a history of working with them, trying to make all these products better. This has always been the focus of Toqué!" Except for mineral water, he takes no deliveries from standard restaurant suppliers. "I started this project twenty years ago, and I'll be doing it still twenty years from now when it's not popular anymore. The work is not finished—it's just starting."

Plenty of other chefs are now in on the project. Have a look around in Lebrun's walk-in fridge and you find the splendid lobes of foie gras from local Le Canard Goulu, along with their whole ducks hung up to age and dry. They keep company in the cold with plump Royal quails from La Ferme Kégo in Cap Saint-Ignace (where owner Gilbert Bernier also harvests sea buckthorn and wild mushrooms for Lebrun). Then there are superb squab from Bellechasse, naturally reared Angus beef from La Ferme Eumatimi, near Drummondville, venison sourced from the Appalachians, and excellent lamb from Kamouraska. Alas, much local seafood sourced from the Gaspé takes a roundabout route to Quebec City, bypassing it on the highway to Montreal, only to be rerouted there at a big distributor like La Mer a few days after it arrives. But Lebrun does enjoy immediate access to farmed Princess scallops from Pec-Nord Gourmet in New Brunswick, snow crab and lobster from the gulf, walleye from Lac Saint-Jean, and even sturgeon caviar from Témiscamingue. There are now too many locally produced farmhouse cheeses of quality to enumerate. What is more intriguing are the wild indigenous plants Lebrun likes to work with, like powderized cattails, the mildly bitter pulverized dried flower of the sumac tree, dandelion honey, wild ginger, and even ice plant—ficoïde glaciale—from his farmer Marc Bérubé at La Ferme des Monts, in Sainte-Agnès de Charlevoix. And last but not least, the extraordinary tomatoes he sources from a retired school principal named Jean Blouin, who lives in nearby Lévis, where in beds fertilized with crushed seashells, kelp, and manure he raises some two hundred obscure varieties of tomatoes (Quebec #13, la Douceur de Doucet,

Opalka, Canabec, le Groseille, Garden Prince, Yellow Flame, and some others as tiny and flavourful as *bleuets sauvages*) and refuses to sell them to anyone but Lebrun, who returns the loyalty.

"Since I got here in 1986," Lebrun recounted, "I've seen a lot of suppliers work very hard to adapt to the demands of local chefs. Today their products are superb, and it's our responsibility to encourage them so that they can make a living from their work—and it's even more important here because the season is so short and the market so limited."

Lebrun is clearly a great believer in the Quebec terroir. But he is my kind of terroir enthusiast: he does not give in to some madcap 100-mile myopia, because he has his eye on the best of everyone else's terroir, too.

"I take the best local products—and if I need to get a product from somewhere else, that's fine too. I'm not going to give up truffles from France," says the French chef who also prefers Bovetti chocolate from Périgord to any other, and correctly asserts that the butter produced from the milk supplied by the farmers' cooperative in Echiré, in Deux-Sèvres, France, is without equal anywhere. "And sometimes it's even okay to be out of season. What's wrong with drying morels in the spring so that you can use them in the fall or the winter? Or preserving cèpes in oil at the peak of their season?"

Absolutely nothing.

～ 7 ～

SMOKED MEAT

My son, Max, is Toronto born and bred, and thus it was not until he was six years old that he was formally introduced to the food of his forefathers—smoked meat. I was freshly returned from Montreal, where, as was my habit, on my way out of town I had stopped in at Schwartz's delicatessen on the Main to collect a whole brisket and all the requisite trimmings—dry karnatzel, sour dill pickles, hot banana peppers, and a few Cott Black Cherry sodas. Following an old routine, around ten thirty in the morning I unwrapped the brisket and sliced off a small taste from the corner of the lean end. It passed. I sliced off another sample just to be absolutely certain. Then, before it was too late, I placed the brisket in my steamer, sealed the lid with plastic wrap and heavy aluminum foil, brought the water to simmer, and—fleeing the irresistible aromas—quit the house in search of some fresh rye bread. I had invited some friends for lunch, and when the first of them turned up salivating at half past noon, I opened the steamer and pierced the brisket with a fork to assess its tenderness.

Adjudging it to be *à point*, I transferred it to the carving board and then ceremoniously prepared for Max his first beautiful sandwich—medium-fat, to get him started on the right track, but a little less of it than you would find stacked between the slices of rye at Schwartz's itself, in deference to his inexperienced digestive system. This thoughtfulness of mine swiftly proved unnecessary.

"Daddy? You write about food, right?" he asked, expressing interest in my career for the first time as he polished off the first half of his sandwich.

"That's right," I replied.

"Then you should write about *this*!" he said, reaching for his second half.

I had written about *this*—several times. I could not help it. For Canada has never produced anything that boasts even a small fraction of the culinary renown of Montreal smoked meat. Our culinary identity abroad is more often rooted in unexciting single ingredients than actual dishes—things like maple syrup and "Canadian bacon" (a minor stylistic rethink of a very common food). And with the exception of poutine, a genuine Quebec original, most of our Canadian cuisine has far too much in common with its European antecedents to appear to others as something new. Canadian pea soup is barely distinguishable from its Dutch counterpart. Even tourtière is just another meat pie, its name taken from a common French baking dish (that story of the extinct Quebec carrier pigeon is apocryphal) and its spicing of cloves and cinnamon borrowed from the traditional English and French meat pies of the era of our early settlers. But while smoked meat also has its roots in Europe, it has followed its own decidedly distinct local course—and to a most excellent conclusion.

The story begins in the Levant, long before refrigeration, where methods of preserving beef and other meats (lamb and goat and just about anything else they could get their dirty hands on) involved spicing, pickling, and air-drying. The Armenians called their version *pastrama*, the Turks made *pastirma*, the Bulgarians *pasturma*, and so on. The Ashkenazi Jews who took their beef-based version of the recipe to New York sensibly thought of steaming the meat to tenderize it, then slicing it and serving it hot on rye as *pastrami*. And while the Montreal take is similar, the primarily Romanian Jewish community who settled there favoured a more assertive spice mix, applied it to a different cut of beef (brisket rather than navel), and—according to the legend of Ben Kravitz, who founded Ben's Delicatessen in 1909—also added a further Lithuanian twist of smoking the meat over smouldering wood chips before steaming it. And even though the smoking part of that original recipe did not catch on, the new name did, and fast. Within a couple of decades, the spiced, brined, roasted, and steamed brisket we now know as "smoked" meat was being sold under that illogical moniker everywhere from the Rogatko deli, which stood beside the Hollywood Theatre at the corner of the Main and Duluth, to Levitt's, Putter's, Schwartz's, and Chenoy Boys. And by the 1940s, hungry people everywhere started to associate the words *Montreal* and *smoked meat* as reflexively as they did *Philly* and *cheese steak, Toulouse* and *sausage, New England* and *clam chowder,* or even *Peking* and *duck.* Montreal smoked meat remains Canada's only contribution to this exclusive pantheon of great dishes irretrievably linked to an identifiable place, and it is highly doubtful that we will ever come up with another.

And that is just one of many reasons why none of the hundreds of other stories I wrote as a staff writer for the *National Post* ever provoked anything close to the response generated by a feature published in the spring of 2003 involving a blind taste test of six different kinds of Montreal smoked meat. The notorious event was conducted at the Rosedale home of Giller Prize founder Jack Rabinovitch, my father's longest-serving friend, from way back at Baron Byng High on Saint-Urbain Street. It was my job to select the delicatessens and order the briskets, and I settled on Charcuterie Hébraïque de Montréal (aka Schwartz's) and Maison du Bifthèque Main Deli (aka The Main) on Saint-Lawrence Boulevard, then Lesters Deli, on Bernard, in Outremont, and finally the newcomers Abie's Smoked Meat, in Dollard-des-Ormeaux, and Smoke Meat Pete, in Île Perrot.

Then Jack and I collaborated on putting together an irreproach-ably impartial tasting panel, selecting names from a pool of friends who shared the unshakable conviction that animal rights began with salt, pepper, and garlic. Being an ex-Montrealer helped, and so did being Jewish—and if you were both, you were a shoo-in. In the end our tasters included Moses Znaimer, the broadcasting visionary who gave us Citytv, agents Michael Levine and Bruce Westwood (Westwood Creative Artists), lawyers Clayton Ruby and Julian Porter, investment guru Gerry Sheff (Gluskin Sheff & Associates), Roots co-founder Michael Budman, Art Shoppe co-owner Allan Offman, York University professor and former Canadian Jewish Congress president Irving Abella, and a handful of journalists—Michael Enright, Joey Slinger, Joe Fiorito, Arlene Perly Rae, and the op-ed director from the *National Post*, my old high school friend Jonny Kay.

I was in charge of steaming the briskets to a state of tender bliss. Then, working on them sequentially, my brother Noah and I sliced each into sandwiches of approximately equal fattiness, cut these into manageable quarters, arranged them on platters labelled only with single letters for coded identity, and sent them out to the dining room for sampling. There, the gathered guests tasted and rated them, and talked amongst themselves in a manner reflective of their sophistication and accomplishment. Which is to say that after the Montreal Jews ganged up on their Toronto brethren to ridicule the quality of their bagels, everyone next got around to discussing the intersection of two hot topics— economics and smoked meat.

"Here's a test of age," Gerry Sheff said, getting that one rolling. "What's the lowest price you remember for a smoked meat sandwich?"

"Twenty-five cents," Znaimer replied, without hesitation.

"I remember thirty cents," Sheff countered. "And Rabinovitch—he remembers two for twenty-five!"

I already knew that to be a fact, because a year and a half earlier, at the surprise seventieth-birthday party my mother had thrown for my father at their flat off Sloane Square, in London, Jack, my father, and one-time McClelland & Stewart proprietor Avie Bennett had gotten into a rousing match of one-upmanship on the identical subject. Meanwhile, in Toronto, as the hours slipped by and the last brisket was carved, the attendees committed their final rankings to scraps of greasy paper, listing the samples in order of preference from first place to sixth (Lesters deli had submitted two kinds of smoked meat—regular and their ne plus ultra dry-aged edition). Then I revealed to everyone which letters corresponded with which delicatessens and began the arduous process of converting rankings into points. For that, I cleverly borrowed the points system then used in Formula 1 racing, which allotted ten points for a first-place finish, six for second, and then four, three, two, and one for the final four positions. But even before I tallied the results, it was clear that Schwartz's would be the victor, for they had placed first on seven of a possible fourteen ballots. In the end that obviously insurmountable lead translated into ninety-nine points, with Abie's in second place with seventy-seven. Smoke Meat Pete came third with sixty points, with Lesters premium brisket close behind with fifty-eight, the final two markers in the distant rear of the field.

The story was published on a Saturday, and the emails began flooding in that same morning, many of them from smoked meat aficionados living in deprived exile. There were letters from overseas, and hereabouts, from as far afield as the Northwest Territories. Everyone had a reminiscence to share; most ventured at least one contrary opinion. One reader pointed out angrily and rather contemptuously that one of the close-up action photographs included with the story unmistakably showed an unidentified hand clutching a knife that was slicing brisket *along rather than against the grain.* (Naturally, I replied without checking that the hand belonged to my brother Noah.) In the immediate aftermath, Jack Rabinovitch told me that more people had complained to him about their exclusion from the guest list that night than had ever done so about not making the cut for the Giller Prize gala. To this day, nearly a decade on, he maintains that his annual visit to his urologist still begins with the good doctor bringing up yet again how he was overlooked on smoked meat night.

But looking back now, it is clear that something important was lost amidst all that controversy: that, what with the small sample size, occasional slicing issues, and other problems of methodology, the twelve-point difference between long-time favourite Schwartz's and the newcomer Abie's was so slender as to be smaller than the margin of error. The future was already foretold.

My paternal grandmother was an unspeakable cook. So more often than not my father's idea of comfort food had less to do with what he had encountered in childhood than with what he learned in later, happier teenage years, when he moved alone to Europe. In other words, for him *tortellini in brodo* trumped kreplach, and with rare exceptions pâté de campagne bested chopped liver. So when it came to my mother's cooking, it never really mattered much to him if she was in the mood to cook something French, English, or Italian; as long as it was rustic and unfussy and did not involve too many vegetables, he was happy as could be. Almost. For even if his mother had been incapable of making a matzo ball soup that was not covered with a slick of yellow chicken fat, or a boiled chicken that did not bounce and jiggle when it made first contact with the knife, there was a small handful of things that she had got right enough to ensure that their flavours still had tenacious reach into his later years. For example latkes, which now and then my mother made for him—sensibly frying them in olive oil instead of schmaltz. Or her uniquely refined *helzel*, for which she used the neck of a goose instead of chicken, marinated its stuffing with a good dose of cognac, and browned it in place of the customary pallor. But aside from these rare exceptions, the Jewish kitchen was not a domain in which my mother cared to venture, not even for him. So on those rare occasions when she travelled somewhere without my father, within half an hour of her departure we were generally in the car and bound for a big delicatessen to stock up on those delicacies that, in addition to declining to cook for him, she discouraged keeping in the refrigerator for reasons of taste, health, and waistline.

So, unsupervised, up at the Brown Derby (on Van Horne) or the Snowdon Deli (on Snowdon) my father would buy heaps of sliced smoked meat, and—for variety—roast brisket, too. He would pick up big tubs of chopped liver, monstrously thick Coorsh salami, ropes of karnatzel, boxes of potato and kasha knishes—and, in his notion of a concession to a balanced diet, some sour pickles and coleslaw. And as soon as we were home he would enthusiastically tuck in. If it was morning, he would toss up one of his signature dishes, a sort of Ashkenazi frittata, which involved many barely whisked eggs, assorted hunks of Coorsh salami and karnatzel, and sometimes a few slices of smoked meat, too, all cooked together in a buttery cast-iron skillet until well set, and then slipped onto the plate with an audible thud, like a small manhole cover. If, however, it was lunchtime or later, my father would put together something a little more substantial. He would begin by popping a selection of knishes into the oven, and while impatiently waiting for them to heat through, slather a vast portion of chopped liver onto a slice of rye, and then assemble a sandwich or two with his smoked meat and roast brisket to plate with the knishes, pickles, and coleslaw. Either way, he referred to the plate he assembled upon our return home as his "Jewish sleeping pill." And sure enough, half an hour after tucking in, he would be contentedly out cold on the sofa.

It was from that same podium that on other days—such as on the occasion of a particularly nasty blizzard of the sort for which school was cancelled even in Montreal—he would rise up on one elbow and bellow to the house at large, "Who is my favourite child?" Any one of the five of us too young to yet recognize this as a trick question (like me) or too slow to get out of sight before being noticed (like me) would be caught in his dragnet, and summoned. And once sofa-side, it would be explained that he was in terrible need of a couple of warming medium-fats from Schwartz's post-haste, but, alas, he was far too busy to make the trek himself. So he would fish some money out of his pocket for a cab and his fix, and dispatch the favourite child (me) or two (usually my sister Emma, for protection) into the howling storm.

This is how, when I was far too young and small to see over the counter at Schwartz's delicatessen (or the snowbanks that lined the sidewalk outside), I met Jan Haim—or Johnny, as everyone knew him. Johnny had arrived in Montreal from Romania in

February 1964, and he had been working at Schwartz's ever since. He started in the kitchen, and by the time I met him was the manager, perpetually stationed at the takeout counter near the front door. When I turned up in those early days, shivering, a little tentative amidst the alarming bustle, Johnny would lean forward over the counter (as far as his belly would allow) and beam a warm smile down my way. Then, whatever the length of the queue in front of me, he would promptly hand me down my father's bag of hot medium-fats. The sandwiches were always ready because my father called ahead—not to make his kids' life any easier, I suspect, so much as to assuage his fears that in our incompetence we might mess up the order and return with a medium or, horrors, a lean sandwich by mistake.

But with the passage of time and age came increased responsibility. Soon, I was permitted to place my father's order by telephone all by myself, which is how I learned that Schwartz's was listed in the Montreal White Pages as the Montreal Hebrew Delicatessen, an entry conveniently appearing immediately below the all-block-letter listing for the Montreal Heart Institute. From there I graduated to placing the takeout order on-site, just like everyone else did. And many years later, when my parents moved from Westmount to downtown, and I was a Schwartz's habitué in my own right, and old enough for my father to take me along to happy hour for company, I would sometimes fetch sandwiches for us all for dinner. Because I had worked out by then that, even though my father adored Schwartz's, he did not much like going there. For despite his special customer benefits— like never having to wait in line, and having waiters offer him a first grab at other customers' french fries as they passed by our table—he did not care for all the attention and preferred to eat at home. I was collecting one such order in 1994, in the middle of a dinner rush, when along with my bag of sandwiches Johnny handed me a copy of my father's just-published memoir about Israel and his school friends who had made aliya, *This Year in Jerusalem*. Johnny told me how much he had enjoyed it, and asked if I could possibly arrange for Dad to sign it. So the next time I visited I brought Johnny back his copy. My father had inscribed it, "For Johnny—The King of Smoked Meat." Wow, did Johnny ever look chuffed. He beamed and his eyes moistened. The sandwiches were on the house.

Emboldened, on a subsequent visit that conveniently corresponded with a lull in the afternoon rush, I asked Johnny if he might give me a tour of the operations out back—the inner sanctum, where the briskets-to-smoked-meat magic unfolded. Many a regular had caught a brief glimpse of the room as the kitchen door swung open and shut, but very little was ever revealed. The Schwartz's kitchen remained a place of considerable mystery and a source of much debate. Some claimed that at Schwartz's the smoked meat really was smoked. Others ventured the contrary, insisting instead that it was brined, like corned beef. "Come," Johnny said, and led the way.

I was jittery with excitement—or at least, I would have been, if I was not struggling to digest two medium-fats. Johnny pushed open the kitchen door and I followed, to discover—well, not much. For while the truth was at last at hand, the most captivating thing about the kitchen at Schwartz's turned out to be that there was hardly anything there. Instead of the expected crazed bustle of a restaurant kitchen, there was only one person on hand. His station consisted of a big sink full of potatoes, a deep-fryer, and that was about it. Where most kitchens have printers spewing detailed orders for the chef to call out to his crew, this single-item operation was equipped only with a bell, obviously linked to the doorbell that I had so often observed waiters pushing just below the cash behind the counter up front. Evidently, a long or a short pulse signalled whether the fries being summoned were for there (on a plate) or to go (in a soon-to-be-translucent paper bag), and the number of bleeps that followed indicated the number of orders required.

One mystery solved; but the bigger one would take more exposition. First Johnny showed me the raw whole briskets. The smallest of them was easily twelve or thirteen pounds—far larger than any that they sell. Johnny explained that they shrink at least thirty percent in the curing and cooking process. The first step is to roll them in Schwartz's secret Bessarabian spice mix until they are completely coated with it. Then the briskets are carted upstairs to the cold room, where they are packed snugly in huge plastic barrels, stacked nearly to the top. They marinate and cure thus for ten days. They begin this process dry, but briskets nearing the end of the curing cycle are completely submerged in liquid. Which technically means that smoked meat is brined. But there is a caveat: no brine is ever prepared, and no liquid is added to the barrels at all. It is simply extracted from the briskets themselves by the salt in the spice mix in which they are enveloped (we are not dealing with quality dry-aged meat here, but rather the cheapest possible raw product, wet-aged in vacuum-packaging, and sodden). Once cured, the briskets are drained and returned to the small kitchen below. There they are tied with twine and hung from a rack. This rack in turn is wheeled into a massive, gas-fired oven, and the briskets are roasted there at a modest temperature (about 275°F) for close to five hours, during which time fat drips onto the flames below and a little smoke is generated—but not so much that you would call the process smoking. Once cooked, the briskets are transferred either to the holding fridge or to the steam table for a final, tenderizing two or three hours—whatever it takes for the meat to yield without objection when pierced with a fork. Now I finally knew the process. All I needed was the recipe for the spice mix.

In the early 1990s my parents sensibly took to quitting Montreal for the winter in favour of far more agreeable Chelsea, London, where, like the rest of the family, I would join them for my Christmas holiday. As the only one of us headed their way from Montreal, I was always charged with a special shopping list. It began with two dozen bagels from the Maison du Bagel Saint-Viateur (aka the Bagel Factory) and a large, whole brisket from Schwartz's. Which is how, late one dark and stormy December morning in the early nineties, I found myself in the eerily empty delicatessen at the unfashionable lunch hour of 11 A.M., sharing the counter with just a handful of others customers—mostly uniformed cops, freshly off shift. I was hunkering down over a couple of medium-fats when suddenly the lights went out. Johnny did not miss a beat: he reached under the counter, produced a candle, lit it, and put it down in front of my plate.

"You know I love Schwartz's, Johnny," I said. "But I have to come clean and tell you that I never imagined I would ever enjoy a meal here by candlelight."

He laughed hard, his belly heaving in the flickering shadows. Then I explained that I needed the usual shipment for my father packed for my flight to London that evening: one well-wrapped brisket of his favoured size of about eight pounds, a little karnatzel, and I was done. So Johnny opened the sliding glass door to the cool alcove inside the front display window and began rummaging around in the stacks of briskets there as if he were searching for a stick of just the right shape in a pile of kindling. Soon he had selected four candidate briskets that looked good enough for my father and appeared to match his weight request, too. But the Schwartz's scale is digital, and what with the power outage, was unusable. So Johnny started weighing briskets in his hands, holding one in each side by side, and hefting them up and down for comparison until he found the one he wanted. "This is a lovely one," he said at last, smiling down at the chosen one. Then he wrapped it in butcher's paper, bagged it with the karnatzel, and handed it to me with a bill for the cashier, handwritten on a piece of greasy paper. I was intrigued to see that according to feedback from Johnny's forearm, my brisket did not weigh eight pounds, but rather, precisely seven and a half.

Back home I wrapped the brisket in an additional couple of garbage bags and taped them up, but I could still smell its rich aroma. So out at Mirabel, fearing that the brisket would provoke a disturbance in the hungry Air Canada cabin somewhere over the mid-Atlantic, I decided to ignore my father's strict instructions to take it carry-on and instead stuffed it into the side pocket of the suitcase that I was checking. Then at Heathrow, I waited and waited by the carousel; no case. So fifteen minutes after the rest of the passengers from my flight had dispersed, I reported the loss to the Air Canada desk and headed for Chelsea. My father took the news badly. For the next two days, whenever the phone rang he grabbed for it with uncharacteristic enthusiasm—and then disappointment crossed his face. Finally, on the third day, Air Canada called to say that my case had turned up at Charles de Gaulle and would be arriving in Chelsea by minicab that same evening. It did, and to our astonishment the blessed French had rejected the smoked meat: it was still there in the side pouch, undisturbed. And what's more, after three days without refrigeration, it was perfectly fine.

"What a beautiful aroma," I said to my father. "They should bottle it and make perfume out of it. Imagine, women wearing a few drops dabbed behind their ears."

He did imagine—and far better than me. For he was writing *Barney's Version* at the time. And when I picked up the novel a few years later, Barney had poached my idea and run with it. "You know if you had really, really been intent on entrapping me on my wedding night, you wicked woman, you would not have dabbed yourself with Joy, but in Essence of Smoked Meat," Barney tells Miriam one night in their happy times. "A maddening aphrodisiac, made from spices available in Schwartz's delicatessen. I'd call it Nectar of Judea and copyright the name."

Meanwhile back in Montreal, Johnny was not doing so well. Three decades of slicing smoked meat was wearing at him. While his belly was as robust as ever, his hair was now white and thinning, and more importantly, his once incomparable slicing arm was on the fritz. After two unsuccessful operations, his rotator cuff remained in apparently irreparable tatters. So in 1998, two years after Schwartz's was sold to its long-time accountant Hy Diamond, Johnny Haim decided that thirty-five years of his life was enough to give to one delicatessen—even Schwartz's—and he retired. It was odd and disorienting walking in and not finding him at his station. But not *that* much—because his son Abie, then a fourteen-year Schwartz's veteran in his own right, took over as manager in his stead. Their physical resemblance was uncanny, so when you walked into Schwartz's there was still a familiar face at the carving station after all.

But then two years later Abie moved on, too, decamping like so many Jews from the old neighbourhood had done before him for the Anglo enclave of the West Island. Which is where, in 2000, he opened Abie's Smoked Meat, in a strip mall on Boulevard Saint-Jean in Dollard-des-Ormeaux. The place does not look at all like Schwartz's. It is modern, spacious, and airy. Instead of ancient, yellowing newspaper clippings, sports memorabilia hang on the walls. But at the back of the room near the service bar you will find a large painting of Johnny in his element: behind a steam table, holding up a large, steaming-hot brisket stabbed on a carving fork, and getting set to carve. The opening of Abie's prompted Johnny out of retirement briefly, and for the first couple of years he dabbled here and there making sure every brisket was *just so*. "One batch of briskets might take two and a half hours on the steam table. Another batch can take just two," Abie explained to me at the time. "Fifteen minutes more or less can be the difference between perfect and near to perfect. And that's where my father comes in, and takes his fork out. He pokes, he prods. And that is the final judgment."

Now and then when I dropped in, I even found Johnny behind the counter, knife in hand, once again hand-slicing the best medium-fats in Montreal. And I say the best with measured consideration. Because a medium-fat at Abie's always tastes just like it used to at Schwartz's in its prime. The raw product is of at least equal quality. The spice mix is identical. So is the process. Even the charcoal grill at Abie's comes from the same supplier and matches the design of the one that Schwartz's used for ninety years (until it was ditched in favour of propane late in the Hy Diamond era). The only major equipment difference at Abie's is that the roasting oven is modern convection, and has digital controls even for humidity levels, so that the product that comes out of it is far more consistent than at Schwartz's, where even in the good years, a dry, salty sandwich was something one encountered more than occasionally.

"In this business," Abie told me once, "you're only as good as your last medium-fat."

But this is far truer for him and other newcomers than it is for an institution like Schwartz's, which despite its cramped premises increases production year after year, and now pumps out more than ten thousand pounds of smoked meat each week. In my experience, the strain of volume shows. When news broke that Diamond had sold the Schwartz's restaurant, building, and condiments business to Mr. Céline Dion and his partners for close to ten million dollars, I did not share others' alarm at the prospect of decline, expansion, and the inevitable Schwartz's outlet at McCarran International in Las Vegas. For decline had set in already, when Diamond expanded takeout operations into an adjacent space on Saint-Lawrence Boulevard, peddling Schwartz's T-shirts and coffee mugs. I actually gave up on the place altogether in the summer of 2009, on the occasion of my fifth consecutive visit rewarded with a subpar sandwich, this one so under-steamed and chewy that I threw it in the nearest rubbish bin in disgust (it was takeout). My last perfect sandwich there was consumed at roughly twelve thirty on September 15, 2007, when the affable manager Frank Silva indulged me with a second Schwartz's first to go with my meal by candlelight with Johnny: he allowed me to *reserve* a table for twelve at Saturday lunch. That sandwich was bliss, and so was the rest of the day (I got married four hours later). It was a great note to end on—and that is the way I like to remember the great delicatessen. And of course I always keep a jar of their steak spice on hand, and can have a sniff when feeling sentimental.

For the steak spice smells almost identical to their briskets. The two spice mixes are obviously closely related. All the same, staff at both Schwartz's and Abie's have long cautioned me for reasons unspecified against attempting to use their steak spice to make smoked meat. And while both delicatessens sell the steak spice, neither sells the brisket mix, and they have always refused me flat out when I begged for some. Until one glorious afternoon in early 2010, when during my customary stop at Abie's on my way into Montreal, I finally had a breakthrough. When I finished up my plate of medium-fats, I had asked Abie once again what the difference was between the two spice blends, and—be it from attrition or some other reason—to my considerable surprise he gave me a proper answer.

"Basically, the brisket mix has a lot less salt," he said. "All you have to do is mix in a bit of water before you rub it on the brisket. Do you want some?" I was barely out the door before I had the cell phone out and was ringing my wife in Los Angeles, where she was travelling on business.

"You won't believe this," I said, feverish with excitement. "But in my jacket pocket I am packing the secret of Montreal smoked meat."

Back in Toronto a few days later, I sat at my desk gazing incredulously at my pouch of spice, feeling rather like Station Chief Strangways must have done once he and Quarrel finally smuggled those rock samples out of Crab Key. Like him, all I needed was a trustworthy lab to do the analysis—and not Professor Dent. Consulting the internet, I settled on Gelda Scientific, a Mississauga lab that specializes in food and beverage chemical testing, and wrote them an email. But the answer that came back was not good: reverse analysis of steak spice was definitely not their thing. However, Technical Sales Manager Damien Boyd did helpfully suggest that I contact Newly Weds Foods, a huge international that specializes in spice mixes, among other things. And indeed Newly Weds eventually got back to me with an offer to duplicate my sample for somewhere between $5,000 and $10,000—but even at that they would not tell me what was in it. (This, I learned, is standard. Revealing the formula would obviate the profit-earning contract to manufacture the duplicate.) Newly Weds suggested that I instead contact the Guelph Food Technology Centre, and so it came to pass that I found myself on the telephone late that Friday afternoon with their manager of business development, Karen McPhee, who was very nice and helpful but had never heard of Abie's delicatessen or even Schwartz's and possibly not smoked meat either, and obviously thought that my request and I were a bit strange.

"Why exactly are you doing this?" she demanded, finally.

"For Jews everywhere," I answered, in a failed bid to clarify things.

Eventually I gave up on modern science and dumped the stuff out on a large sheet of white paper in my kitchen, pulled it apart grain by grain, and examined it with a magnifying glass borrowed from the drawer of my boxed *Compact OED*. What I could not identify by sight I tasted, and in a short time I had an ingredients list: cracked black pepper, chili flakes, crushed coriander, yellow mustard seeds, caraway or possibly dill or fennel seeds, garlic flakes, onion flakes, and a whole lot of salt. I mixed up a batch, added a little water, and rubbed it all over a nine-pound dry-aged brisket freshly procured from my butcher, Cumbrae's. Then I rubbed the Abie's spice just as tenderly all over the control brisket (same size, same supplier). I placed each in a separate container in preparation for their stay in the cold room. "You don't flip them, nothing," Abie had said to me. "You just leave it for ten

My Montreal Smoked Meat

The odd fact of the matter is that even the most authentic Montreal smoked meat is not smoked: it is instead brined, and then slow-roasted, and then steamed. This recipe gives smokier results. If you prefer something more akin to the product at, say, Schwartz's, simply cut back on the smoking time, and exchange it for an equal amount of time in the oven at the same temperature.

1/3 cup (75 mL) kosher salt
1/4 cup (60 mL) cracked black pepper
1/4 cup (60 mL) yellow mustard seeds
2 tbsp (30 mL) cassonade or other brown sugar
1 tbsp (15 mL) saltpetre
1 tbsp (15 mL) caraway, dill, or fennel seeds, toasted
1 tbsp (15 mL) garlic flakes
1 tbsp (15 mL) onion flakes
1 tbsp (15 mL) chili flakes
1 tbsp (15 mL) hot paprika
1 tbsp (15 mL) dried juniper berries, crushed
1 beef brisket, fat cap on, about 10 lb (4.5 kg)

Combine salt, pepper, mustard seeds, sugar, saltpetre, caraway, garlic flakes, onion flakes, chili, paprika, and juniper berries in a bowl, add 2 tbsp (30 mL) cold water, mix well, and let sit for 5 minutes. Place brisket in a casserole or some other container, spread half the spice mix on the top side, flip, and cover the second side. Cover container and place store at 50°F (10°C) for 8 days (a cold room is ideal, but you can also use your second refrigerator set at its lowest possible setting).

Smoke the brisket, flipping it periodically, at 275°F (140°C) until the internal temperature reads 170°F (75°C)—5 to 6 hours. Transfer to the rack of a steamer and steam until the meat yields easily when pierced with a fork—about 2 hours. Slice against the grain and serve on rye bread with mustard.

Suggested side dishes: Jewish sorbet (sour pickles) and coleslaw.

days and let nature do its beautiful work." When I finally cooked them, the control brisket was terrific, and my first effort was very tasty and nicely textured—but inside it was brown, like roast or barbecued brisket, instead of sporting the characteristic pinkish red hue of Montreal smoked meat. I stared at them side by side and thought hard. Suddenly I remembered that brisket of my father's that got lost in Paris without a refrigerator for three whole days yet emerged unscathed. Only one preservative could ensure that: saltpetre, which preserves colour as well as the meat. I had the formula at last.

8

RISE AND FALL
OF THE TASTING MENU

A year after it opened in August 2000, Susur Lee's restaurant Susur defined itself with an untraditional stance from which it did not retreat until the day it closed in 2008: the restaurant would operate without menus. Technically, there were two small exceptions. Diners were indeed presented with a sheet of paper that theoretically invited choice—but the carte was not much larger than a business card, and the information proffered there empowered them to choose only between a full blind tasting menu of seven or more courses, or an abbreviated version that ran for only five. That aside, the only menus printed were to commemorate special events to which the diner was already committed—say, something designed around the occasion of a visiting chef like Ming Tsai, or Ken Oringer, or merely according to the whim of chef Lee, who was given to stirring up media interest (and business) with themed banquets commemorating such events as the arrival of Chinese New Year. The last time I dined at Susur, he was putting on a special tasting menu in celebration of the freshly arrived first harvest of the treasured black truffle of Périgord.

Lee was at the door when I arrived. Already in his late forties, he remained trim and fit, a heritage possibly of his youthful immersion in the obscure martial art of Baguazhang (which translates as the equally incomprehensible "eight-trigram palm"). He greeted me warmly and directed me toward a private corner of his stark white restaurant, where I sat alone in a booth for four alongside the kitchen doors. I looked out on the room from beneath Susur's loudest design feature, an inset light box of perpetually changing colour. My view of the room was framed at left by the restaurant's western wall, which featured an under-lit shelf that ran its entire length, and always featured a display of odd kitschy dolls that Susur's wife, Brenda, had tracked down on eBay (and then lost on Gay Pride weekend, when customers invariably pocketed a few). On the occasion of my last visit the dolls were the same as on my first: a vintage set created in the ghastly likeness of a chef considerably less imaginative, fit, or stylish than my host, but immeasurably more famous—Colonel Harland Sanders.

Even without the market penetration of KFC, Susur Lee is the best-known chef this country has ever produced. London-based *Restaurant* magazine named Susur one of the fifty best restaurants in the world, and in New York, *Food & Wine* once anointed Lee one of the ten best chefs working anywhere. Some years ago, in Kyoto, I walked alone into what was supposed to be the best restaurant in town and sat down at the bar. The old sushi master stationed there prepared for me at least a dozen sensational courses, seemingly doing his best to raise the ante with each one and to finally concoct something too squiggly and weird-looking for a white person like me to eat (raw shrimp carcass, slivered raw sea bream skin, octopus roe, etc.). Then to my surprise, in defeat he revealed that, despite his earlier uncomprehending shrugs and protestations, he could, in fact, speak some English—and asked me how I had come to be enjoying an omakase menu in his restaurant. Too full to come up with a better explanation, I told him the truth: a randomly consulted hotel concierge had sent me over, after I arrived in Kyoto via bullet train from Nagoya, where I was attending the world Expo with a chef from Canada.

"The name of the chef?"

"Susur Lee."

"*Ah!* Susur!" he said, smiling broadly. Then he disappeared into his back room, and a few minutes later returned with a photograph of Lee beside one of his recipes in a cookbook, and flipping a few pages forward, showed me that he, too, had a recipe in the same volume. My host turned out to be Yoshihiro Murata, one of the best-known chefs in Japan, the very man Joël Robuchon turns to when he needs culinary advice on things Japanese. He made me stay for as many more courses as I could handle, an interminable tea ceremony, then cigars, and I almost missed the last train back to Nagoya—all because he and Lee had once cooked together in Singapore.

Lee gets around. Before starting my truffle menu at Susur, I asked him how he could possibly have procured winter truffles from Périgord so early (it was the first week of December; the harvest begins at the earliest at the end of November and does not peak until late January). Lee told me that he was fresh back from Frankfurt. There he had cooked with chef Mario Lohninger, who owned the nifty nightclub Cocoonclub, with an adjoining restaurant called Silk and a tasting room named Micro, where every dish was served as a single, bite-size portion on a spoon to a diner who—like Nero or Caligula—ate and imbibed while reclining on a sofa or chaise longue. And while in Frankfurt, Lee had met a purveyor of unseasonably early winter truffles, and opted to purchase a couple of kilos and smuggle them home in his carry-on luggage.

Lee's meal started with an amuse-gueule of miso-flavoured custard set in a tiny rectangular dish topped up with a shallow pool of quail consommé, a small dollop of Ontario caviar, and a scant few truffle shavings. When you sampled a small spoonful of custard, the soup rushed in to fill the fresh cavity in the dish, and the caviar was instantly beached. When you ate the caviar and custard together you encountered a clever trick of mouthfeel: the flan provided a soft, silky textural contrast to the roe that made the eggs feel firmer and more distinct than they would taste on their own. That was typical Susur alchemy—making a second-rate product like that slightly mushy Ontario caviar taste firmer and better than it was, almost like the real thing.

Next, Susur served his main course, for he liked to serve his courses in a progression of decreasing size and impact, a concept he called the "reverse tasting menu," and believed that he had invented (although I should point out that in *The Physiology of Taste*, published in 1825, Brillat-Savarin wrote that "the proper progression of courses in a dinner is from the most substantial to the lightest"). Here we had a fillet of venison loin roasted rare, sitting on its end in a pool of rich, black truffle sauce. Its neighbour on the square plate was a globe artichoke cooked so gently and for so long that each petal was as tender as the flesh at its base. The choke had been displaced in favour of a stuffing of sweet duxelles. The next course was the inevitable foie gras served in a predictable multitude of iterations—one small escalope, seared, one dome of foie gras mousse set over foie-gras-infused sabayon. At the other end of the rectangular plate, a thin slice of cured, truffle-infused duck magret rested on a warm salad of goat's cheese and sunchoke. Next, a breather of guava sorbet sitting in a pool of lemongrass-spiked mango-pineapple juice. Upon landing on the table, the sorbet disappeared briefly in the swirl of heavy mist emanating from its bed of dry ice, temporarily transporting the Susur experience to some Polynesian theme restaurant of yore—in my case, to the Kon-Tiki lounge in Montreal's Sheraton Mount Royal Hotel.

Next, Susur took a jaunt to the sea, with caramelized sablefish, skate cheek, crab, shrimp, salted duck egg, and dashi-poached winter melon heaped together in a vaguely gooey, superior stock-style clear broth, like some sort of Chinese bouillabaisse. The black truffle shaved overtop provided an earthy undertone, offset in the end by the mild bitterness of the winter melon. Next, there was a firm mousse of Japanese scallop moulded in the shape of the muscle from which it was cast, nestled anew in its former home—its shell—the top of which has been decorated with petals of edible flowers, and the inside dressed with two butter sauces, one laced with truffle, the other with tarragon and chives. Then came a creamy gratin of B.C. honey mussel, topped with truffle, next a salad of mâche, roasted pear, and truffle vinaigrette, and finally, a course of sweet dim sum.

A year later, Lee left the game of haute cuisine, so that meal was emblematic of the style with which he finished. The plates displayed an assertively artistic sense of composition and colour. Asian influence showed itself conspicuously in the chef's preoccupation with mouthfeel. But in the flavour equation, the Asian inflections that earned Lee his original renown were increasingly relegated to a supporting role. To come clean, I far preferred it when the duelling cuisines of his particular French-Chinese fusion were mated the other way around, with—if you will—the Chinese on top, for his exposé of unusual Chinese flavours and textures was far more compelling and singular than his takes on new European cooking ever were. But then, as Lee put it to me once, European flavours went better with those expensive bottles of wine he was counting on selling.

Lee was born in Hong Kong in 1958—the Year of the Dog. He was the youngest of two boys and four girls born to an accountant father and an illiterate mother who worked as a tea lady at the local British army barracks. Lee cites his mother's frightful cooking as an early inspiration to pursue a career in the kitchen. He also had a precocious sense of taste—he claims that when he was only six, and his mother made him an after-school snack, he could tell the difference between fresh rice, rice reheated from the day before, or a mixture of the two. He remembers vividly as a child falling asleep to the sounds and aromas of the hawkers' stalls set up across the street from their tiny government-subsidized flat on Castle Peak Road. On Chinese New Year, his father would take him to the celebrations at his employer's house in Hong Kong Central, where, confronted with the unfamiliar wealth of choice at the celebratory banquet, young Lee would behave like a college freshman at a keg party, gorging with abandon, only to get sick from the excess on the long bus ride home to Kowloon.

"It happened about six times," Lee once told me. "My mother would get so mad at me."

His appetite did not extend to academics, and at fourteen, Lee dropped out of high school. He moved in with his brother, Michael, and took the first job he found: as a bar boy at a restaurant called Me Lai Trin. Only a few weeks later he was fired for getting into a fist fight with a co-worker. But he had already recognized in himself an interest in the professional kitchen; it was not just the food preparation, but the life. "They could swear and throw things and tell the waiters off, and I thought, 'That's where I belong.'"

Next he took on the job of dishwasher at the (still) wildly popular Peking Garden restaurant in Kowloon, where aside from scrubbing however many woks it takes to feed three or four hundred customers each night, his duties included gutting fish, peeling shrimp, shucking oysters, and poaching lobster. A year or so on, a friend told him of an opening for a better-paying, drier job at one of the Western-style hotels, and so it came to be that in 1974, sixteen-year-old Susur Lee signed up as a stock boy at a place he had never heard of: the Peninsula Hotel.

"When I first walked in to the kitchen at the Peninsula and heard the chefs speaking French, it sounded to me like they were throwing up," Lee told me of his first encounter with the language of Molière.

He persevered, not with the language but with the food—the vast, strange, and utterly foreign cuisine that I was brought up to think of as *l'art culinaire*. Gaddi's, the showcase restaurant at the Peninsula, was a formal French restaurant with a conventionally organized European kitchen. It took Lee three years to make chef de partie, and then chef saucier, in which capacity he soon found himself stationed in the restaurant proper, pushing his trolley around the grand old dining room and finishing sauces with a theatrical, flaming-booze-embellished flourish for all to see. And that is how, while flambéing up a steak au poivre one night, he met a visiting English teacher from Tillsonburg, Ontario, named Marilou Covey. A year later he quit the colony for the first time to go travelling with her, and via a deliberately circuitous route through Southeast Asia, India, Egypt, Morocco, Greece, Italy, and France, finally made it to Toronto in September 1979.

For Lee, cooking was then just a job, and he signed up for three: he started his day baking croissants at an uptown patisserie, then did a dinner shift as a line cook at the Sheraton Hotel, and then another at a nightclub in Yorkville. When Covey took a course at the University of British Columbia, Lee landed a gig cooking pasta at a restaurant owned by Umberto Menghi. Later, back in Toronto, he returned to French cooking, but this time in the novel and intriguing form of *la nouvelle cuisine*, when he signed up as chef saucier under Gunter Gugelmeier at the

Westbury Hotel. Other French restaurants followed, but Lee showed no signs of finding his culinary voice. They had married and were planning a return to Hong Kong when, on September 1, 1983, Covey perished along with 268 other passengers and crew when a Soviet jet fighter shot down Korean Air Lines flight 007. In the grip of depression, Lee stayed put and signed up for the easiest job he could find: flipping burgers at a place called Peter Pan, on Queen Street West. The local talent pool was slight and he was soon offered control of the kitchen.

The Queen West strip was then the city's only neighbourhood to possess some reasonable fraction of New York–class gritty, stylish, urban cool. As Lee began to look around at what was happening, he perceived that the local clientele might be willing and eager to try something new. To begin, he marginalized the burgers and pushed salads and other healthier fare to the fore, sometimes making references in taste and texture to his Asian roots and other times to his French training or his recent travels. As the months went by, Lee began to demonstrate several proclivities that would from then on figure prominently in his career. His willingness to experiment by merging seemingly disparate elements of his training and experience into a new and successful whole was foretold in his first hit dish: a first course of a French-inspired chilled soup composed of a purée of watermelon and rhubarb (if you are Chinese, cold soup is dessert). The authoritarian streak of kitchen discipline that later earned him a reputation for throwing a lot of well-aimed pots and pans got off to a good start when he slapped a joint-puffing sous-chef with an open-palmed blow that extinguished the spliff right on his face.

And his habit of frequent travel to seek inspiration from other cultures and other restaurants was established when Peter Pan's owner, Larry Guest, increasingly enamoured of his suddenly well-known chef, allowed him to take a month off each summer.

Pretty soon Lee was seeking ideas not for that restaurant but his next one—his own, which he wanted to open with a Peter Pan waitress, his new girlfriend and future wife, Brenda Bent. They opened Lotus in 1987. Over the next decade, Lee used that thirty-five-seat room to establish that his particular melding of French and Asian culinary traditions was one of the most simultaneously daring and coherent expressions of fusion happening anywhere. Then in 1997 he closed the place, packed up his young family, and quit town for Singapore, where he opened a restaurant named Club Chinois for the TungLok restaurant group, and worked as their consulting chef-at-large. When he returned two years later to look for a space for a new Toronto restaurant, he was determined to build one with a kitchen that could allow him to demonstrate all the new techniques he had learned in Asia—right down to steam ovens for cooking and heating individual bowls of soup. He also wanted to show off newly familiarized Asian ingredients. And the best way to showcase as much of each as possible was to build it with a kitchen large enough to enable what he tried to do but could never properly manage from the tiny kitchen at Lotus: multi-course tasting menus for every customer.

The blind tasting menu is a modern hybrid of two long-established culinary traditions: the French *menu dégustation*, that formal, luxurious, multi-course affair, meticulously scripted with punctuation by amuse-gueules, sorbets, and *mignardises*; and the

Singaporean Slaw with Umeboshi Dressing

Chef Susur Lee

Serves 4

For the pickled red onion
1 cup (250 mL) rice wine vinegar
1/4 tsp (1 mL) black peppercorns
1/4 tsp (1 mL) kosher or sea salt
1/4 tsp (1 mL) fennel seeds
1 sprig thyme
1 bay leaf
1 red onion, julienned

For the umeboshi dressing
1 cup (250 mL) umeboshi (salted Japanese apricot) paste
1/2 cup (125 mL) rice wine vinegar
3 tbsp (45 mL) granulated sugar
1-1/2 tbsp (22 mL) onion or chive oil
1-1/2 tsp (7 mL) minced ginger
1 tsp (5 mL) dashi broth
1 tsp (5 mL) mirin
Salt

For the salad
3 cups (750 mL) corn or peanut oil
1 shallot, thinly sliced
1/2 taro root, peeled and julienned
2 oz (55 g) rice vermicelli, broken into 3-inch (6 cm) pieces
2 green onions, julienned and soaked in ice water
1 large English cucumber, seeded and julienned
1 medium carrot, julienned
1 small jicama, peeled and julienned
2 large Roma tomatoes, blanched, peeled, seeded, and julienned
2 tbsp (30 mL) peanuts, toasted and crushed
4 tsp (20 mL) sesame seeds, toasted
4 tsp (20 mL) fennel sprouts

4 tsp (20 mL) purple basil sprouts
4 tsp (20 mL) daikon sprouts
4 tsp (20 mL) edible flower petals

For the pickled onion, combine the vinegar with 1 cup (250 mL) cold water in a saucepan and bring to a boil. Add the peppercorns, salt, fennel seeds, thyme, and bay leaf; simmer for 5 minutes. Pour hot over the onion in a bowl and let steep for 1 hour.

For the dressing, combine the umeboshi paste, vinegar, sugar, oil, ginger, dashi, mirin, and salt. Purée. Adjust seasoning and set aside.

For the salad, heat the oil in a deep saucepan to 325°F (160°C). Add the shallot slices and fry until bronzed and crisp—about 2 minutes. With a slotted spoon, remove shallots to paper towels to drain. Salt lightly. Raise heat so that oil reaches 400°F (200°C). Add taro strips and fry until bronzed and crisp— about 2 minutes. Remove to paper towels to drain, and salt lightly. Add the vermicelli and remove it as soon as it curls—about 2 seconds. Salt lightly.

To finish, scatter vermicelli on 4 plates. Drain the green onion, pat with paper towels, and scatter over the vermicelli. Follow with the cucumber, carrot, jicama, tomatoes, and pickled red onion, mounding the heap into a peak. Sprinkle with peanuts and sesame seeds, and finish with a scattering of fennel, basil, and daikon sprouts, flower petals, and the crispy shallots. Serve the dressing on the side.

Japanese tradition of omakase, wherein the customer honours the chef with his trust, carte blanche. It was Anton Mosimann who, in 1981, put the two together to come up with his *menu surprise* at The Terrace in the Dorchester Hotel. And—unsurprisingly—it later fell to Charlie Trotter, a thinking chef and a jazz enthusiast, to popularize these culinary jam sessions in the States from his Chicago base. Vancouver chef Rob Feenie had done an apprenticeship with Trotter in the early nineties, and it was on a return visit to Trotter's kitchen in 1997 that he was inspired to give his struggling young Vancouver restaurant, Lumière, a rethink.

"Lumière opened November 11, 1995," Feenie said, telling me the story some years later. "We were à la carte. And French. Going through some papers the other day, I found a menu. A rack of lamb was $21.95. We did veal with morels, *filet de boeuf* with peppercorn sauce. People complained it was too much like Le Crocodile. They were right."

There was not much to choose from in Vancouver in 1997—"Umberto's, Le Crocodile, Bishop's. That was it"—but two versions of one of them was still one too many, and so Feenie decided to revamp the Lumière concept with a big nod to Trotter, and in particular to those blind tasting menus that would eventually help catapult the American chef to ten James Beard Foundation awards and two Michelin stars. And for Feenie, who was the first chef to perform the tasting menu trick in Vancouver, the ensuing adulation was similar, in large part because as well as being new to town, the format was so very liberating for his cooking.

"I cook by taste. I cook by experiment," he explained to me. "I grew up with Japanese food, and later, in France, with French food. I'm not going to cook Indian food—I like to stay in a comfort zone of what I know. Lumière was an Asian-influenced restaurant with French techniques."

The small-plate format suited his instinct for tidy juxta-positions of those two traditions because by their very nature, uncluttered by the other elements that must be included in a conventional main course, small plates lend themselves to the clear assertion of a single culinary point. Tasting menus also proved to be a dazzling showcase for Feenie's unrelenting finesse. I was lucky enough to enjoy many of them. One of the last started with a demitasse-sized portion of a velvety purée of sweet corn enthusiastically sprinkled with white truffle oil. Then there was scallop tartare made with thin, delicate slices of small bay scallops built in a little mound over a raw oyster, enhanced with the mild crunch of a fine brunoise of blanched celery, dressed with vanilla-infused trout roe, foamed onion jus, and the very surprising but eminently successful addition of a few shavings of pecorino. (When I asked how he had ever thought of that one, he came clean: "Actually, we didn't plan it and we didn't used to make it that way. The cheese fell off another plate at the pass, and instead of taking it off the tartare, [chef] Marc-André [Choquette] said, 'Let's try it!'") The next course was a tiny, delicate *boudin blanc* served atop a bed of orzo laced with shredded lamb cheek and a reduction of red wine and lamb jus so rich that it left one's lips tacky. Then there was sablefish, glazed with soy, ginger, and sake and plated with braised pork belly and tiny, delicate chanterelles, all encircled with a shallow moat of truffled vinaigrette. And finally a few slices of ultra-tender duck magret accompanied by a delicate ravioli stuffed full of shredded confit, sauced with a duck reduction laced with smoky paprika, its citrus notes an echo for the two tiny, peeled segments of clementine perched on top of the magret. As usual my notes then trailed off into generic observations on rich Quebec cheeses and impeccable desserts.

Feenie's tasting menus were a success from the outset. In 1997 *Vancouver Magazine* anointed Lumière the best restaurant in Vancouver. In 1998, the first year that Lumière began to focus exclusively on tasting menus, *Foodservice and Hospitality* magazine named it "Canadian restaurant of the year." The next year, *Gourmet* magazine named it the best restaurant in Vancouver, and the year after that, Lumière became the only free-standing Relais Gourmand in Canada (joining two Quebec hotels, L'Eau à la Bouche, in Sainte-Adèle, and the Auberge Hatley, in North Hatley, in what was then a small Canadian club of three to boast the top Relais & Châteaux designation, since renamed Les Grands Chefs). Then in 2001, Lumière joined an even more exclusive club: Les Grandes Tables du Monde.

"I'm calling you to tell you this," Feenie told me when he reached me on my cell phone, "because no one I've called in Vancouver has even heard of it."

It had been growing apparent for some time that Feenie's Lumière was increasingly operating at a disconnect from the tastes of his small hometown. His restaurant had no hope of charging the same prices as his sister restaurants in Relais Gourmand and Les Grandes Tables du Monde, places like Le Gavroche in London, Le Bernardin in New York, or Pierre Gagnaire in Paris. But he carried on all the same. Across town, West had opened with David Hawksworth at the stove, on request turning out tasting menus of equal calibre, course for course. Multi-course *menus dégustations* accounted for more than half the meals prepared by Normand Laprise at Toqué! When Susur restaurant opened in Toronto in late 2000, written tasting menus were popular at all the top restaurants in Toronto—Splendido,

North 44, Scaramouche, The Fifth, Canoe, and Avalon. By the time Perigee opened in the Toronto Distillery District, in 2003, serving nothing but blind tasting menus, chef Susur Lee was doing that and more—his blind tasting menus were running ten or more courses.

The format was a godsend for chefs inclined to one-upmanship and showing off (i.e., most of them). And at a time when fine dining of genuine quality was a new phenomenon, freshly arrived in cities like Toronto and Vancouver that had been anything but weaned on it, it was the perfect framework with which to introduce diners to new flavours and ideas of which they would not ordinarily partake. For no matter how enthusiastic the consumer, there would always be more customers at David Hawksworth's West ordering fish and chips at lunch than those selecting an appetizer of raw and cooked sea urchin with fennel. The same held true for Feenie's braised sweetbreads with truffled lentils, and Marc Thuet's braised calf's brains with foie gras and his navarin of spring lamb with its kidneys and testicles. Even chef Susur Lee's unusually dedicated diners were not going to make his elk strip loin with slimy *yamaimo* (Japanese mountain potato), arame (seaweed), and uni (sea urchin gonads) or Chinese-style braised abalone with braised pig's ear, celery, and black truffle salad the bestselling items on his menu. And if these chefs and others like them had not put these dishes in their tasting menus, they would instead have languished in some overlooked corner of the printed menu, until they were excised from it altogether the following month to make way for something more accessible and profitable—which is what restaurants are all about.

So for food critics like me who ate out too much, our palates jaded and bored somnolent by the prospect of another perfect veal chop with porcini and cream, the tasting menu and all the nifty flavours that came with it were more than welcome. As long as they were executed by the right hands, they made for the best possible night out. After a time, though, it did begin to dawn on me that I was probably guilty of praising some of them in a manner that exceeded their particular relevance. A lot of people simply did not care to eat that way. Svelte women in particular seemed to consider the tasting menu a form of torture. And when I think back to some of those twelve-course dinners turned out by Susur Lee or some other chef who had asked me what I considered then to be such a lovely question—"May I cook for you?"—it is not always my full belly I remember from the experience so much as my bruised shins, courtesy of my date across the table, hissing, "Please, make him stop," and kicking me under the tablecloth every time the waiter turned up with yet another course to explain.

The public's enthusiasm for tasting menus was well on the wane long before the sinking economy struck its fatal blow in 2008. Although Feenie would not prove able to hang on to Lumière long enough to see the necessary changes through (he was ousted in late 2007), he had told me in 2006 of his plans to drop his tasting menu format and revamp to satisfy more casual tastes. By then, back in Toronto, Perigee had gone to a conventional menu format, only two or three percent of diners at North 44 were choosing the multi-course option, and Splendido owner Yannick Bigourdan had assured me that his were still popular only because hardly anyone else did them any longer. Susur himself was giving up on the concept the year before he formally wrapped it up with the closure of his eponymous restaurant that was so entwined with it.

"The bottom line is that there's a new generation in my restaurant now," Lee explained to me in late 2007. "They want to experiment but they want to have an element of familiarity with what's on the plate, or they don't remember what they've eaten. People don't want to sit for so many hours anymore. They don't want to spend the same big money."

By then, neither did I. But for the rarest exception I had grown bored with the procedure, too, and did not see why chefs who could not get their point across in three or four courses should be indulged with another hour of my time to try again. Worse, the corrupting habits of learning the cooking trade in kitchens focused on tasting menus were starting to percolate into restaurants run by the younger generation: time and time again, I would try out some new place, have a great first course, and then be stumped by the second one—and in particular, by what the young chef had decided to plate with the protein. It started to dawn on me that most tasting menu kitchen alumnae had no idea what went well with what because they had never seen it done before—small plates do not have side dishes. It was fun for a while, but the time had come to turn the page.

Some form of tasting menu or *menu dégustation* nonetheless endures in Canada, at institutions (like Toqué!, in Montreal), at new restaurants where serious young chefs are cooking at their own restaurants for the first time (like Michael Caballo at Edulis, in Toronto), and elsewhere by special request. The Japanese tradition of omakase is alive and well at serious Japanese restaurants (like Sushi Kaji, in Toronto, or Tojo, in Vancouver). But by and large none of our chefs enjoy the co-existing circumstances that enable their counterparts stateside to continue more successfully with the format. American chefs simply have greater celebrity and international draw, and in cities like Los Angeles, New York, and Chicago, they enjoy a combination of local wealth and throngs of tourists seeking culinary experiences at any price that nowhere here can match. All top New York restaurants, such as Daniel, Per Se, and Jean-Georges, continue to offer extended menus. In Chicago, Grant Achatz's tasting menus at Next! are sold out months in advance, and a reservation at his all-tasting-menu Alinea is also hard to come by. Nevertheless, even in Chicago, Achatz's one-time mentor Charlie Trotter announced earlier that he is withdrawing from the game, closing his flagship eponymous restaurant after a twenty-five-year run in order to return to university to pursue a master's degree in philosophy. (He never was an ordinary chef.)

The trend in Canada is to get back to basics on the plate—and to maximize profits through the use of a good name. No one has been busier at this than Susur Lee, who in 2008 finally made good on a fifteen-year-old threat to quit Toronto for New York, when he seized a last-minute chance to open a restaurant for the Thompson Hotel group in their new property on the Lower East Side. Lee called his hundred-seat New York outpost Shang. The next year, Lee opened a second restaurant for the Thompson group, ostensibly saving the day by filling in when

Todd English unexpectedly backed out of their new property in Washington, the Donovan House. And in early 2010, he rejoined forces with his friend Andrew Tjioe's TungLok restaurant group and lent his name to their new restaurant, Chinois by Susur Lee, in Hotel Michael at Resorts World Sentosa in Singapore, which he is required to visit three times a year. Back in Toronto, in 2008 his old flagship, Susur, was first relaunched falteringly as Madeline but lasted only two years (it was perhaps never a good idea to name a restaurant after a mother you tell everyone was a terrible cook). Madeline's became Lee Lounge, an adjunct to his original mid-range restaurant, Lee. Like Lee, Shang and Zentan were never in the tasting menu business. They also marked Susur Lee's return to the predominantly Asian flavours with which he made his reputation. Even so, Shang was poorly reviewed and closed in 2011. Zentan was better received, and continues to do fair business. In Singapore, Chinois serves upscale new Chinese cooking with great success.

In Vancouver, meanwhile, Rob Feenie lost Lumière in 2007, settling in next as the food program director for the Cactus Club Café chain.

9

DESSERT

Faced for the first time with the long drive past the ugly clusters of fluorescent-lit automobile dealerships that litter the Harbourside district of North Vancouver, only to have the taxicab pull up in front of an ugly strip mall, I paid up and disembarked with the sinking feeling that there had been some sort of ghastly mistake. It was not the driver's, though—it was the chef's. Still, while Thomas Haas Fine Chocolates and Patisserie occupies a decidedly ugly, remote, and peculiar setting, it is equally evident that locals in possession of a discerning sweet tooth have been very quick to forgive the man.

When I first visited his shop, lunch hour had barely begun, and already customers were pressed up against the counter two or three deep, clamouring for cappuccinos, croissants, *danoises*, croissants *amandines*, brioches, and pains au chocolat. A few opted for the daily sandwich. But most proceeded directly to what was supposed to come next, what had really brought them here—dessert. Say, the Haas take on the classic *tarte au citron*, which he calls "lemon lemon tart in shortbread crust," or the Stilton cheesecake with rhubarb compote, or the princess cake (white chocolate mousse with light lemon cream and a coconut almond biscuit), or the Manjari chocolate cake (with Manjari chocolate mousse and rum-spiked Manjari chocolate crème brûlée), or the almond and mascarpone cake (light mascarpone cream over soft almond sponge cake with amaretto and coffee). Some customers were taking it easy—with a couple of his famous Chocolate Sparkle cookies, or a small, hand-picked selection of his house-made chocolates.

Chef Haas was evidently enjoying the commotion—his habit of planting himself cheerfully at its epicentre was conspicuous. A buoyant, youthful man, he gave a compelling impression of being everywhere at once. When I first walked in I spotted Haas through the window of the swinging door behind the cashier, mouthing unheard instructions to his all-female crew of *chocolatières*. Then, in the blink of an eye, he was behind the counter, bobbing this way and that, extending a hand to greet one customer and then another, then starting their individual orders, disappearing through the kitchen door again to fetch something essential, only to return and engage a new customer afresh. The girls stationed behind the counter with him were picking up the slack and finishing the orders he had started without to-do. They were obviously used to the routine, however dizzying it appeared from the vantage of the shop floor.

The public area of the Haas patisserie is cramped and modest. Walk in and you are confronted first, dead ahead, with the current Haas raison d'être, the crux of this business—chocolate. The large, glass-fronted display case shows a beautiful array of elegantly presented little chocolates in every sensible contemporary flavour that a refined addict could ever long for (yes to cardamom, no to tarragon and spruce). Some are coloured red or yellow, others are embedded with gold, none are gaudily overwrought. The boxes that you could fill with your selection are displayed on shelves on the left wall, and their design is value-added, another expression of the refined Haas aesthetic. Only the small ones are of conventional flat and rectangular form; opt for any selection greater than twenty-seven in number and the chocolates will be packed into a multi-level home of three floors or more, each one hinged to pivot outward independently of the others, so that if the variety you most desperately wanted was on the bottom level, you need not disturb the neighbours upstairs to get at it. The design for his chocolate bar packaging is equally clever, but in this case mainly for its deceit—because it looks to be packing twice as much chocolate as it really contains.

Chocolate is the crux of the business. Thanks to online ordering, the customer base spans far and wide. On the off chance that you have ever wondered to yourself if Barack Obama, George W. Bush, Bill Gates, and Alain Ducasse all had something in common, take it from me—they do. For although Haas refuses to confirm it, and instead insists that discretion and quality should alone speak for his brand, I have it from a very reliable source that his chocolates have been served for years at the White House, Microsoft HQ, and select Ducasse restaurants. The Haas client base is varied and sizeable enough that he orders and processes roughly eighteen tons of raw chocolate each year. His sources are

Valrhona of France and Felchlin of Switzerland. Haas does not roast, winnow, or conch a single bean of his own raw cacao. "Why should I? It's so labour intensive. I think that someone who does four hundred times as much work like that does not always get a better product. I prefer to rely on the expertise of the chocolate maker—as long as they source fair trade beans and, like Valrhona, conch for seventy-two hours, so it is perfectly smooth."

Conching is a process that was invented in Switzerland in 1871 by Rudolphe Lindt, by which coarse and granular chocolate paste extracted by the winnower is slowly stirred in a vat with rotating paddles or blades until rendered smooth. Additives such as sugar, vanilla, and cacao butter can simultaneously be blended in. The combined effects of heat friction and pulverization of solids eventually yield a liquefied product of undetectably minuscule particles. The process also exerts chemical changes, rounding out the flavours inherent to the beans, eliminating acidity, bitterness, and other unpleasant top notes until the mix arrives a supple, silken whole. In other words, long conching makes for consistency, and is thus one of the principal reasons why Valrhona's basic chocolate (rated for strength, rather than identified by individual plantation) tastes as identical from one year to another as does, say, a bottle of N.V. Veuve Clicquot, regardless of variable external factors (like source and weather). That sort of consistency is ideal for making boxed flavour chocolates, wherein the chocolate is a vehicle for added flavours in the filling or the mix. If you want to instead showcase the complex flavours of individually sourced beans, exhaustively long and homogenizing conching is not necessarily the way to go.

Enter David Castellan, the only Canadian *chocolatier* I know of who disagrees with Haas about whether making your own chocolate is a good use of one's time. Like Haas, Castellan is a pastry chef by training, and in the nineties filled that role very ably for Marc Thuet at Centro Grill & Wine Bar. Then he moved on to a succession of restaurants in the Oliver and Bonacini Restaurants group (like Canoe and Jump). In 2001, with the blessing of his employers, he decided to take a short leave in California to enrol in some chocolate-focused courses at Richardson Researches, a culinary school near San Francisco (it was subsequently folded into the University of California at Davis).

"My goal was to learn panning—it's the oldest machine in confectionery," Castellan explained to me. "But when we were there we also made chocolate from scratch."

And that was that. Suddenly, the panning machine that applied chocolate coatings to nuts and their ilk was no longer so very exciting. Cacao bean roasters, winnowers used for coaxing pure cacao nibs from the raw fermented bean, and conches for turning their paste into smooth chocolate were suddenly everything. So Castellan changed his focus from full-fledged desserts to pure chocolate, and dove in. He went home to Toronto, found a location in the old brick-paved Distillery District, and got to work on opening a small artisan chocolate shop. He called it Soma—the Latin equivalent of the Greek *theobroma*, which is the name of the genus of all cacao-yielding trees.

Theobroma and *soma* mean "food of the gods," but in those early days Castellan toiled on a very mortal scale. So much so that he was unable to locate a cacao roaster small enough to suit his modest needs—or fit in his shop—and thus was obliged to purchase a coffee bean roaster. They are not interchangeable: Castellan calibrated it to its new task by slowing its speed of rotation (to lessen the oil-extracting impact on the oily cacao bean) and lowering its generated heat (for the cacao bean requires a long, slow roast to purge its high moisture). And as no one manufactured a winnower suitably sized for a cottage-industry chocolate maker either, Castellan manufactured one himself. Where industrial machines could extract nibs from a ton of roasted cacao beans in one hour flat, his machine took all day to process fifty kilos. Only then was it time for conching.

"It was so hard to get cacao beans back then," Castellan recalls of a time when brokers were unaccustomed and disinclined to doing small-scale business. "When we got our two or three bags direct from Venezuela it was so precious. If we dropped a bean on the floor we'd actually go scurrying after it. The chocolate and the process was so expensive we thought we'd never be able to make it work."

To supplement the business of selling his own bars, Soma ordered chocolate from Valrhona just like Haas, to turn into truffles with different centres, other flavoured chocolate, gelato, and so on. And with a surprising swiftness word got around the Toronto restaurant scene that Soma's house-made chocolate was top quality and highly distinctive. Thuet bought it for his pastry chef Bertrand Alépée at The Fifth, and later for David Wilson at his Bistro and Bakery. Oliver and Bonacini restaurants were investors in the Soma start-up and did their part to help make it work on the sales side, too. Soon the little shop expanded into new quarters next door.

When I last visited Castellan, in the spring of 2012, he was fresh back from a fact-finding mission to Japan with his wife, Cynthia Leung, who designs all the packaging for Soma products as well as the shops in which they are sold. A second Soma outlet had opened on King Street West at Spadina Avenue the previous June, a bakery was next in the works, and the noisy, dirty part of his chocolate production—the roasting and winnowing—had been moved to a third site, deep in the west end at Roncesvalles Avenue and Dundas Street. Out there he was operating on a whole new scale, processing about 150 kilos of beans every week with new purpose-built machinery. In particular, he had just acquired a classic German roaster from the 1940s called a Barth Sirocco. (It was previously the property of the award-winning chocolate maker Scharffen Berger, whose operations in and around Berkeley, California, were wound down after its 2005 sale to Hershey's.) But despite the increased capacity, he was more focused than ever on making chocolate tasting bars of single-origin beans of distinctive character, which get conched behind a glass display wall in the Distillery District shop for an average run of fifteen hours—but sometimes double that, and sometimes less.

"Conching is mysterious and times don't tell that much," Castellan cautioned, as we sat over espressos at a table alongside the display window. "Conching time depends a lot on the exact process and the type of machine. With top-quality cacao you never want to over-conch, because it removes top notes. What I can say is that we roast our single-origin beans at a very low temperature of about 250 to 260°F"—300°F is more common-place—"to preserve character. The precise amount of conching time is a decision you have to make as you go, like blending whisky or kneading and baking a loaf of bread."

Procuring beans of quality from different origins is far easier today that it was when Castellan started. Once confined to Venezuela, Soma now sources from Ecuador, Java, Bolivia, Peru, Mexico, Java, and just about anywhere where he is convinced that the fair trade label is honest. En route home from Japan, he had even stopped in at a five-hectare start-up plantation in Hawaii. The tasting bars he produces from the beans are assertively pure, restricting ingredients to cacao, organic cane sugar, and cacao butter, and excluding the customary additives of soy lecithin and vanilla. He blends them all to the same 70 percent purity, to encourage the tasting of different origins side by side. And doing so is pure pleasure. Alto Beni, from wild Bolivian cacao trees, is singularly creamy, with a hint of dark molasses. His beans from Java yield an unusually pale chocolate with fruity notes and a trace of smokiness. The beans for his Guatemalan bar are grown by an indigenous tribe in Cahabón in the Alta Verapaz mountains; the chocolate tastes pleasantly earthy, with notes of ripe berries. Another, from the Dominican Republic, boasts a hint of tobacco. Or at least that's what I thought of them at first—but I keep second-guessing myself and going back for another taste just to check.

Back in Vancouver, meanwhile, the shelves alongside Haas's chocolate bars are crowded with ingenious products he has created with his blocks of Valrhona and Felchlin. A glass-fronted refrigerator is packed full of another Haas marketing success story: ready-to-bake-at-home varieties of his stupendously (and deservedly) popular chocolate truffle cookie, the Chocolate Sparkle. Then there are a host of hot chocolate mixes by the tin, chocolate-covered citrus peels of varied interpretations, and fruit jellies. The aforementioned *viennoiseries,* cakes, and tarts are all displayed behind glass at the main counter, on the far side of the chocolate display, where Haas was stationed.

I asked him to select for me something archetypically Haas, and he stopped moving for a good ten seconds of rigid contemplation of his current offerings. Then, without consultation or any further ado, it was decided that I should sample his pistachio and sour cherry tart. One of the sales personnel was instructed to make a cappuccino for accompaniment, and then Haas looked around his bustling shop for a place to put me. The four stools crammed in on the counter's right flank were occupied. There were four more lined up at the windows to either side of the front door, overlooking the parking lot, but only a single perch was free in either row. It was in any case too noisy in there for undisrupted conversation, so Haas told me to take a seat outside and wait for him there. By the time I slipped out of the shop, he was there already, clearing the dishes from a table for us and wiping it down—and then he disappeared again. There were four or five other plastic tables on the narrow sidewalk, wedged between the front of his shop and its designated parking slots; one near me was occupied by an SUV, the overhanging nose of which was pressed against my chair. The other tables were half-full, most of the customers young and female. None of them was the tiniest bit overweight or showing any hint that such a fate might be lurking in her imminent future. Vancouverites—they probably cycled here, I thought as I took a long sip of my cappuccino, its topping of foamed milk prettily streaked and patterned in that way that no one ever seems to have the time to bother with back East.

My focus shifted to the cherry tart, and it looked promisingly fattening. It had a pastry shell of standard buttery shortbread crust—just like you would find on a lemon tart. The sour cherries were set in a thick, light green pistachio cream and, in turn, capped with a luscious-looking dome of pale mousse, lightly glazed so as to sport an enticing sheen. Shards of toasted pistachio had been scattered overtop, and around the periphery, in the gap between the outer edge of the mousse dome and the surrounding crust, five paper-thin strips of shiny dark chocolate had been affixed to the glaze. I carefully cut off a forkful of the tart containing every visible component, and was working on it when Haas returned and took a seat across from me.

"I didn't know that you were licensed," I said.

Haas smiled but said nothing.

The patisserie is not licensed, of course, but all the same it must be noted that, like so many other German and Alsatian chefs whose work I have happily sampled, chef Haas will never be accused of short-pouring when it came to the kitchen speed rail and his marinades and pastry fillings. Simply put, if you passed some of these tarts around at an AA meeting, you would soon be responsible for dispatching a shocking number of the crowd down a road they ostensibly no longer wished to travel. The sour cherries had been marinated in cognac until soused, and the dome of mousse compounded this boozy state of affairs, for it was a chantilly cream heavily spiked with kirsch, the clear brandy made from sour cherries. And what a lovely mix: the pastry was crisp and buttery; the cherries both sour and rich with the flavour of brandy; the pistachio cream provided a backdrop of rich nuttiness; the chantilly added a mildly bitter almond-like note from the cherry pits in the mash that made the kirsch; its glaze packed a citrusy tang; the pistachio slivers added a crunchy counterpoint; and the hint of chocolate brought it all together with flavour notes that were the perfect balance of bitter and sweet—about sixty percent cacao, I guessed.

"Sixty-two percent," Haas corrected me.

The craft of the pastry chef is by necessity highly precise, and the product of this particular set of calculations was profoundly enjoyable—but not definitively so. Our expectations of great desserts have evolved considerably over the past two or three decades, and are no longer established by the corner pastry shop, whether it be some run-of-the mill Just Desserts or Dufflet outlet in Toronto, coasting on locals' sentimental childhood attachment, or even the real thing, like Lenôtre, Dalloyau, or Ladurée in Paris. Because no matter how exemplary your preferred patisserie might be, its staff will inevitably sell you a ready-made dessert, and as such, it cannot compete with a plate assembled just for you *à la minute* in a top-quality restaurant any more than a pizza that spent thirty minutes in a takeout box will taste as good as one delivered to your plate directly from the brick oven.

Think, for example, of the classic upside-down apple cake, tarte Tatin. A pastry shop, even a very good one, will make a large tart, and very likely sell it to you already righted—which is to say with its bronzed apple filling showing and the pastry beneath already growing soggy from the syrupy runoff from the caramelized apples. But in a decent restaurant, they would make it for each customer by the portion; in a fine restaurant, the pastry would be cooked separately to ensure a perfect state of flakiness, and only at the very last moment before being sent to your table would it meet its topping of impeccably arranged braised apple and be paired with, say, some freshly churned ice cream or something of that ilk.

Some decades back, the great Paul Bocuse proclaimed that one could always judge a restaurant by its lemon tart and crème caramel. No coincidence, then, that back in the eighties, when the young Marco Pierre White was advancing English standards in his quest for Michelin stars for his restaurant, Harveys, he decided that as his restaurant was open for lunch and dinner, his lemon tart should be cooked not daily but instead twice a day—one batch before each service, to be served in its prime. Is there a pastry shop anywhere that will serve you an *à la minute* tarte Tatin or a lemon tart so incontestably fresh that it is still warm and fragrant from the oven? No. And that will always be so—or at least, it will remain thus until the day your corner pastry shop can charge twenty dollars per portion, and then reliably talk you into an extra C-note's worth of espresso, cognac, and mineral water on the side. So pastry chefs in charge of pastry shops will forever toil in the shadow of their fellow pastry chefs who work in the restaurant business and continue to put together those plates that raise the bar. And while Haas is no exception, there is an irony to that because he himself was in his last life a restaurant dessert chef who did as much as—and often more than—anyone else in the business when it came to elevating our expectations of the final course.

"It's such a different energy working in a restaurant kitchen, and I loved the high pressure of it—the fact that it's just got to be done," Haas said, leaning back in his chair, his brown eyes widening for a moment at the recollection. Then, looking down at what remained of my cherry tart, he added, "Plated—I would do that differently. The process, the way you do it, it's all different. I would do it *à la minute*. The pastry would be much smaller, more delicate. There would be other components on the plate … "

The Haas tart of the Thomas Haas Fine Chocolates and Patisserie era was lovely; but the plated restaurant desserts on which he built his reputation were more than that. They were magical. And they still are when he turns his hand to them.

Confectioner's sugar—*puderzucker*—runs thick in the Haas blood. Back in 1918, which was not a big year for starting new businesses in Germany, Thomas Haas's great-grandfather finally realized a dream and opened Café Konditorei Haas in his hometown of Aichhalden, in the Black Forest. Eventually, his son took over the family business and became its master pastry chef—the *konditormeister*. Then it passed to the next generation, and by age ten, young Thomas, too, had begun the unofficial training

Pineapple Carpaccio with Ginger Vanilla Syrup and Cilantro

Chef Thomas Haas

Serves 6 to 8

1 ripe pineapple, peeled
Leaves from 1/4 bunch cilantro
1/4 cup (60 mL) granulated sugar
1/4 cup (60 mL) simple syrup
1 tsp (5 mL) finely grated ginger
Seeds scraped from 1 vanilla bean
3 tbsp (45 mL) lime or lemon juice

To finish
Lime sorbet
Diced mango and fresh raspberries (optional)

Slice the pineapple as thinly as possible—on an electric slicer, a mandoline, or with a very sharp knife. Muddle together the cilantro and sugar. Combine the simple syrup, ginger, and vanilla seeds in a bowl and begin adding the lime juice until the desired level of tartness is obtained. Arrange 6 or 7 overlapping slices of pineapple on each chilled plate. Sprinkle them with the cilantro sugar and drizzle with ginger vanilla syrup. Top with a quenelle of lime sorbet—and, if desired, a scattering of raspberries and diced mango.

that it was presumed would one day allow him to take over the business. It began, of course, with washing dishes. By age twelve, he was lending a helping hand with arranging the pastries. But by the time he reached sixteen, his father had decided that Thomas should not serve his formal apprenticeship at Café Konditorei Haas; father thought son would learn more, and learn it better, elsewhere. Thomas complied, decamping for a pastry shop in nearby Gengenbach, where he spent three and a half years, and then to the town of Karlsruhe, near the French border, where he found work at the Confiserie Endle. "They are still two of the best patisseries I have seen anywhere," Haas said.

The collective experience unfolded precisely as an apprenticeship ideally should—at least, for such a motivated student. "There were new tasks all the time, new things I had not done before, and I had to learn a lot of them by myself. The benefit is that [at that age] you don't have any fear of exploring different ways of doing something new until you get it down. Let's say you've never made a tarte Tatin in your life. You look it up in three good books and it's all different. You have to try them all." This process of learning by experimenting within the framework of tradition continued apace for four years, and then, at age twenty-two, Haas was made *konditormeister* at the Confiserie Endle. He concedes now that he was "way too young" to take on the job; his perception of his inadequate training for the position is one of the principal reasons Haas today describes himself as "self-taught."

Next, travelling on a Rotary Club of Germany scholarship, Haas wound up in Brazil, where he instructed young local chefs in the German technique of the chef patissier. Upon his return to Europe in 1993, he made the jump from the pastry shop to the posh Swiss restaurant kitchen, courtesy first of the Hôtel Belvédère, in Davos, and next at the two-Michelin-starred restaurant Jöhri's Talvo, in St. Moritz. In February, at the peak of ski season, this exclusive alpine resort plays host to the St. Moritz Gourmet Festival, and it was an accident of this particular event that set Haas on course for North America. One of the perks afforded the posh clientele of the festival is that they may ride by calèche around town, stopping at any or all of the participating restaurants. And among those who stopped off for a little dessert at Jöhri's were the general manager and executive chef of the Four Seasons Hotel Chicago. And they liked what they ate. They liked it a lot. "They asked for me to meet with them, and then they handed me hiring papers under the table."

As with so many other young European chefs struggling with the cost of living in the Old World, America had already figured in Haas's plans, and so he accepted the offer on the spot. And then, like so many others before him, he was refused an American work visa, and in the pinch, settled for the place next door: in 1995, Haas was named executive pastry chef at the Four Seasons Vancouver. In 1997, he took his Four Seasons team to New York City to compete in the North American Pastry Chef of the Year competition, and they finished in the top three. In 1998, they did it again. Among those who took notice was the renowned chef Daniel Boulud, who enticed Haas to New York City to serve as his executive pastry chef at his flagship Restaurant Daniel, which he was then about to relocate to the Mayfair Hotel and the recently abandoned site of his former employer, Le Cirque.

The new and improved Restaurant Daniel opened in December 1998 to a flurry of accolades (*New York Times:* "four stars"; *International Herald Tribune:* "top ten in the world") in which Haas played no small part. But the routine pace of the working life at a restaurant operating at this lofty level quickly began to wear on him. Workdays typically started at seven in the morning and ran to midnight, and often later. It was an unpleasant challenge for his young family. "I picked up my daughter when I got home and she barely recognized me," Haas has noted many times, sometimes even venturing that he was so unfamiliar to the baby that she was actually scared of him. Meanwhile, New York did little to quench his taste for the unadulterated outdoors and the sports that went with it. Thinking about Vancouver again, Haas decided that in the end it might be more enjoyable to be a big fish in a small pond rather than the other way around.

So in 2000, Haas quit Restaurant Daniel and returned to the West Coast to open a business of his own: Thomas Haas Fine Chocolates and Pâtisserie. To help pay the hefty bills for all that hideously expensive equipment particular to the pastry kitchen (proofers, vacuum emulsifiers, tempering and enrobing machines, Robot Coupe blenders, Tekna coolers, Ecolab sanitation systems, and more), he also took a job as pastry chef at the Metropolitan Hotel, looking after its restaurant Diva at the Met, as well as dessert and chocolate operations sold under its café and restaurant brand name Senses. "Senseless," he calls it now that the relationship is over. But it must be mentioned that in 2001 he took his Senses team to the Valrhona National Pastry Competition in Los Angeles, and they placed first in the chocolate category, first in design, first in sugar—and took the prize for first overall, too, because that was the only category left.

It was in 2003, at Lumière in Vancouver, that I first sampled a plated dessert prepared by Thomas Haas, and to come clean, when I noticed that his contribution to the meal was imminent, it inspired a certain dread. Nine other fabulous courses had already come and gone, most of them conceived and prepared by a sensational guest chef visiting under the aegis of the Relais & Châteaux—Santi Santamaria of the three-Michelin-starred Can Fabes, near Barcelona. And as Santamaria had finished his run with a dessert of his own—*raviolis de frutas tropicales con mascarpone*—my palate was a long way from complaining that the kitchen had left anything unsaid. My belly was equally satiated, straining as it was under the recent influx of oysters, scallops with slivered pig's ear, two-way lobster, rockfish *en crépinette*, confit of duck, and foie-gras-stuffed squab—not to mention my ill-considered decision that afternoon to take a late lunch nearby at Memphis Blues, where the slow-barbecued pork side ribs and beef brisket had turned out so well that I had decided to follow up with an order of Cornish hen. In short, when the Haas item finally came up on the schedule, a second dessert looked to me like overkill no matter who was going to be making it. And when I consulted the menu to see what it was going to be, hoping for something tiny—or even better, something dry that could be discreetly slipped into a jacket pocket—I discovered rather gloomily that Haas in fact intended to send out not one dessert but two, and intended to follow those with petits fours and finally the *mignardises*.

The first dessert was a salad of sage-scented winter fruit (peeled segments of sweet clementine figuring most prominently) served with feather-light parfait of yogurt and a bracing lime sorbet. It proved to be so startlingly refreshing that my slumbering appetite was roused once more, and my curiosity sufficiently piqued to get me out of my seat and off to the kitchen to watch chef Haas plate the next course. This one was a crispy chocolate napoleon plated with caramel-poached Anjou pears, coconut sorbet, and vanilla *gelée*. I finished every exquisite morsel. The execution, the attention to detail in the individual components, and chef Haas's exquisitely light touch in balancing his principal flavours with subtle counterpoints made for an experience I had seldom even come close to encountering on the dessert plate, and it left me wanting more. No small achievement under the circumstances— and I learned over the intervening years that he can perform the trick again and again and whenever he wants, all because it is essentially impossible to eat so much as to be uninterested in a final course of his celebrated and supremely refreshing pineapple carpaccio with lime sorbet and cilantro.

"These signature dishes from our past repertoire that are such crowd-pleasers, these are what I do at special events," Haas explained that day to me on his café terrace, when I inquired about the state of public access to his plated desserts now that he has left the high-end-restaurant business.

That night, for example, he was booked to prepare desserts for six hundred at the launch party for the latest Audi A6. This, after his customary 7 A.M. start and a typically hectic service at the patisserie, from which he also operates an internet and telephone mail-order boxed-chocolate business that sees him plough through about eighteen tons of raw Valrhona chocolate every year. Obviously, Haas is doing good business in the only field a pastry chef can go his own way after leaving the formal restaurant trade. And the fact that he counts the White House and Alain Ducasse among his customers must be pleasing. But all that satisfaction aside, one is obliged to question how the pace at Thomas Haas Fine Chocolates and Patisserie can be much of an improvement on that of Restaurant Daniel that he worried was leaving him estranged from his young daughter.

"It's the same shit," Haas said of his new hours, smiling as always. Then he conceded that earlier that spring he had suffered herniated discs and had subsequently felt for the first time that he was burning out. He followed with a health cleanse, abandoned caffeine, and made a minor adjustment to his six-day-a-week, 7 A.M. to 10 P.M. schedule by giving himself three hours off each Wednesday morning to go mountain biking. "I take baby steps. I cannot change drastically—I would not be capable to do that."

Evidently not: not long after that conversation, Haas opened a second retail branch in the far more pedestrian-friendly locale of Kitsilano, on West Broadway—although in a nod to the home life, he resisted public pressure to open it for business on Sundays. Shortly thereafter he admitted to a friend that he had just cracked a tooth while playing hockey.

"No big deal," his friend told him. "It happens all the time."

"I didn't have the puck," Haas clarified. "No one hit me."

He was just standing on the blue line, clenching his teeth with a little more than his customary intensity.

10

THE NEW CUISINE

Late in the second week of the 2010 Winter Olympics, when Vancouver's secret was irretrievably out of the bag and the whole world knew that it rained there all the time, I checked in with Rob Feenie to see how things were going for Cactus Club Café restaurants, the (then) seventeen-restaurant chain he had joined a few months after losing his baby, Lumière, and its adjacent bistro, Feenie's, in late 2007. The chef was not answering his phone, so I sent him some very brief questions by email, and the replies came back promptly—typed out in short form on his iPhone, with a new subject heading inserted into my original email: "INSANE."

How were sales in the Olympic town?

"One million in three locations."

What about sales of his signature butternut squash ravioli?

"Twenty-two hundred pieces yesterday."

Mini burgers?

"Fourteen hundred in two locations."

Feenie grew up in the hamburger-friendly Vancouver suburb of Burnaby, "like Glenn Anderson and Dale Walters," with two brothers and a sister. His father was a fireman; now and then, when young Rob visited him at the station, he agreed to Rob's repeated pleas to let him slide down the pole. He was an athletic child, adept at both hockey and soccer, and he harboured hopes of a professional sports career. This meant a lot of afternoon practices, after school and on weekends. "Coming home [on Sunday] there would always be a roast and Yorkshire pudding. I still like roasting meat, mostly because of Mum and Sunday night. Okay, so she overcooked everything—but I just loved that scent." Burnaby provided him with only one striking exception to overdone roasts and sliced white bread: the Feenies' neighbours hailed from Osaka. "I played with them. I ate with them. Every New Year's Eve, they had the best teriyaki chicken wings you've ever had. I'm still trying to duplicate them. I loved their food."

His next formative food experience came under the aegis of the local Rotary Club exchange program, whereby at age seventeen, Feenie quit for Sweden for a long and busy summer. "I had no idea what Europe was about. I went ice fishing, sailing, diving for mussels. I saw World Cup soccer in Germany, I went to Spain, Italy, and France." European life—and the food that fuelled it—was an "eye-opener." He still recalls vividly the richly flavoured coffee, breakfasts that strayed from the customary formula of cereal, eggs, and bacon in favour of cheeses, ham, *filmjölk* (a Swedish take on yogurt), and *smörgas*—open-faced sandwiches that were never made from pre-sliced white bread, but instead with something crusty that was fetched fresh each day from the local bakery.

Feenie returned to Vancouver with evolved tastes and interests. A professional sports career still had appeal but was no longer a likelihood, and so it came to be that in 1983, with his eye fixed exclusively on immediate financial benefit, and unequipped with any specific knowledge of the professional kitchen other than once having heard mention of Paul Bocuse, Feenie took a kitchen job in a North Vancouver restaurant, long since defunct. "In Burnaby, a lot of my friends, well, they thought I was a fag," Feenie told me once of how this news went over in the suburbs long before anyone had ever put together the words *iron* and *chef*.

Undeterred, and finding unexpected pleasure in the work, Feenie signed up for classes at Vancouver's Dubrulle Culinary Institute and two years later graduated with his Red Seal certificate. He next worked his way through apprenticeships at restaurants around the province, ending up eventually at what was then the flag-carrier for French haute cuisine in Vancouver, Le Crocodile. There, Alsatian *chef-patron* Michel Jacob quickly assumed the role of mentor to young Feenie in much the same way as many years before, the great Émile Jung, of the original crocodile—the Michelin three-star Restaurant Au Crocodile in Strasbourg—had done for him. And as Jacob was a product of traditional French culinary training, he foisted the same system on Feenie, encouraging him to work his way up through the hierarchy of responsibilities at Le Crocodile by staggering that progress with *stages* at kitchens around Europe. And especially in Alsace, where Feenie did time under the three-Michelin-starred

Antoine Westermann as well—of course—as Jung. "Michel gave me two months off to work with his mentor—and then when I came back he wouldn't let me work nights anymore," Feenie recalls, of Jacob's mixed feelings about his protégé's growing skill set. More apprenticeships with top American chefs followed; Feenie did stints with Charlie Trotter in Chicago, Daniel Boulud and Jean-Georges Vongerichten in Manhattan, and Thomas Keller in Yountville, California. Finally, in 1995, Feenie opened his first restaurant, Lumière, on West Broadway in Kitsilano.

Two years into its slow start he staked its place on the culinary map with an all-tasting-menu format that would eventually lead to Lumière's being named *Vancouver Magazine*'s Restaurant of the Year for an unprecedented seven years running. In 2001 he added the casual Tasting Bar alongside, and in 2003, borrowing a page from so many notable Parisian chefs, he opened an accessible and affordable bistro (named Feenie's) next door to his flagship. And then in late 2007, just two years after becoming the first Canadian to triumph on *Iron Chef America* (over the redoubtable Masaharu Morimoto), Feenie lost it all. He was pushed out of the two restaurants he founded by a new business partner who ultimately preferred the allure of high-priced and high-profile rented talent from New York, in the (short-lived) form of Daniel Boulud.

It took some months for Feenie to land back on his feet, and when he did so, in the test kitchen for the Cactus Club Café restaurant chain, many of those who followed developments in the culinary community were shocked. For Feenie's Lumière had shone with unusual intensity; in my well-nourished opinion, the restaurant enjoyed two or three glorious years round about 2001 when it was certainly the best in this country—and easily as good as anything you could find elsewhere. Then all of a sudden the Iron Chef had a new Cactus Club business card sporting the silly moniker of "restaurant menu architect." The new assignment involved improving everyday grub for commoners who ate enough fish tacos and chicken Caesars to drive sales across the seventeen-restaurant chain north of an annual $100 million. Many saw shame in the comedown. But much as I missed Lumière even then, it did also occur to me that one could just as convincingly make the opposite case. Which is to say that striving to create the perfect $15 hamburger to satisfy thousands of hard-working bellies each week was at least as lofty a calling as conceptualizing precious tapas-sized portions of things like butter-poached lobster with lobster bisque and mascarpone risotto, dishes conceived to merely tease the appetite of an over-privileged few.

In 2008, when Feenie set to work reinventing that hamburger, changing beef suppliers and designing a highly specific ratio of ground chuck to ground sirloin and ground fat, Cactus was already selling close to 250,000 burgers per annum. Today they sell considerably more. Since Feenie came on board, Cactus Club has added six restaurants to its portfolio (such as their new ne plus ultra outlet on lovely English Bay), and as I write, there are plenty more on the imminent horizon—like at Coal Harbour in Vancouver, and on Adelaide Street in the Toronto financial district, their first Cactus outlet east of Alberta, scheduled to open in late 2012. But when, one afternoon in 2010, I lunched with Feenie at Bentall 5, then the $6-million flagship of the Cactus chain, it was not the burgers that interested me. Of course I tried one anyway, and also had a polite bite of his excellent club sandwich (with Cantonese-style barbecued duck) as well as his hunter's chicken. But my visit of culinary inquiry really hinged upon the butternut squash ravioli with truffle beurre blanc, amaretti, pine nuts, and crispy sage.

I had first encountered the dish nearly a decade previous, when a scaled-down portion of two or three ravioli had appeared (briefly) before me as part of a long, three-figure tasting menu at Lumière. We next met a couple of years later at the Lumière Tasting Bar, and then once more, next door at Feenie's. But while Feenie's was meant to represent the chef's idea of casual, this latest venue for his classic dish was something else again. Behind its massive glass wall on Burrard and Dunsmuir, Bentall 5 has seating for more than three hundred diners and drinkers spread over two levels. The place never empties out between seatings. Any direction you turn, your gaze will fall on an enviably fetching waitress hustling past, delivering more drinks and hot plates. When Feenie and I settled into our booth for our 2 P.M. lunch, the restaurant was still at least half-full from the lunchtime rush. Back in the days of the Lumière Tasting Bar, Feenie sold about four hundred ravioli (sixty-five plates of six) each week. Now over the same time period he was instead overseeing weekly sales of about fifty thousand ravioli (7150 plates of seven, at $17.50 per) across the Cactus chain. And I was keen to determine how, aside from price, the dish had changed as its purpose evolved from pleasing a discerning (okay, wealthy) few to instead satisfying the rapacious hunger of the masses (well, middle class). I wanted to know how quality had been compromised to quantity—and whether it mattered.

To look at the plate, not that much had changed. It was at first glance the same old cluster of delicate, domed, hand-cut butternut-squash-stuffed ravioli, pleasantly drenched in beurre blanc. They had been finished with a sprinkling of truffle oil, toasted pine nuts, and crisp-fried sage. In the good old days tiny cubes of black truffle had been stirred into the sauce and glistened seductively in the buttery emulsion. But unsurprisingly that pricey brunoise had since been swapped out for truffle oil, a far cheaper delivery system for the same lovely aroma. The next most prominent difference was snapped into focus by the excess of pepper freshly deployed direct from the mill by a well-intentioned if over-exuberant waitress.

One of the things you pay for in a restaurant of the calibre that Lumière once possessed is the presence of an expert chef at the pass, constantly tasting and prodding and making sure that every plate is up to snuff, its seasonings in perfect harmony, before it leaves the kitchen. There is obviously no time for that sort of thing at a place like Cactus Club. But most diners are oblivious and ambivalent. Do you think that your average mildly demanding male diner prefers the knowledge that just before his plate left the pass, a brilliant chef just stuck a spoon or finger into the sauce to ensure that it was just so? Or would he prefer a little fantasy-provoking interaction with a gorgeous, peppermill-toting waitress with an effortlessly warm smile, asking him if he would like some more pepper on his dish—even though he has not yet even tasted it? As the waitress retreated, I naturally put this question to Feenie.

"Some people miss the truffles," he replied, displaying his seldom-observed diplomatic side. "The filling is exactly the same.

The dough is exactly the same. The sauce and the garnish ... no."

The recipe for the filling really is the same. Ditto the pasta. And the man who puts the two together in an industrial kitchen in the Vancouver suburbs does it with the same moulds Feenie used to use for the purpose in his own kitchen. The fact that the ravioli are next frozen before being shipped to the various Cactus outlets changed nothing in the equation, for these squash ravioli were always frozen before being cooked at Lumière, too (it prevents the dough from being dissolved by its moist filling). The difference in the saucing is that, while back at Lumière it was always a *true* beurre blanc—which is to say nothing but butter, emulsified in an acidic reduction of wine and vinegar—here, of necessity, the finicky sauce was instead stabilized with cream (an old trick of which restaurants far more expensive than Cactus invariably partake). Then there were the absent truffles and—arguably—some diminished finesse in the plating and garnish. Finally I had a bite. Feenie's synopsis was correct: the pasta that was once rolled out and cut by hand in his kitchen and was now prepared by commission in someone else's remained as good as it always was. The filling of drained squash mixed with mascarpone (omitting the traditional thickening bread crumbs of its Tuscan progenitor) was just as rich and velvety as it always had been. Most palates would not pick up on the cream in the beurre blanc. And if I missed the truffles, I would still on most days rather pay $17.50 for the dish at Cactus than double that for the old dish with a little *Tuber melanosporum* added in.

Feenie has spent the intervening years making over the rest of the Cactus menu, to such an extent that the little circled "RF" that

Cactus prints alongside the Feenie-designed dishes on the menu are now in such majority that the few pre-Feenie favourites that linger on are isolated like lepers. One lunch menu I saved from Bentall 5 has eight features—and only one, a steak with mushrooms and mashed potatoes—lacks the Feenie stamp of endorsement. The important thing is that Cactus is a good place to eat. So much so that, given what has happened to the economy and our best high-end restaurants since Feenie made his surprising jump there in 2007, his move has a way of in retrospect appearing prescient. High-end dining as we knew it has been in precipitous decline, for the struggling economy accelerated an evolution of taste that was already in play. For as we have grown increasingly accustomed to eating well, and more confident that we are doing so, it was inevitable that we should have less time, use, or desire for the pretentious and aspirational trappings of Old World formality.

One thing that has happened is that with North America's increased confidence in the abilities of our own chefs, more and more informed consumers correctly dismiss pretentiousness for what it is, and want no part of it. There is for me no better example of this than what happened in New York to Alain Ducasse, when even before 9/11 and the economic downturn he opened in the Essex House, with preposterous prices justified with flourishes of service that extended to diners being offered silver trays bearing dozens of Montblancs, Cartiers, and other pricy writing implements to choose from in order to sign their bills. There was a time when Americans might have been impressed or even intimidated by such a spectacle if they had encountered it in Paris. But in the comfort of home, just five years shy of seeing some of their own chefs anointed with three Michelin stars, New Yorkers already knew that they did not need Ducasse around to teach them anything culinary. Critics and customers laughed Alain Ducasse at the Essex House out of business in, well, a New York minute.

The second development I credit to the legacy of the gastropub—by which I mean a *real* English gastropub, not the sad pretenders that wear the label here. For when you have the chance to sit down at a place like The Kingham Plough, in Oxfordshire, and settle in with a plate featuring a grilled cutlet of spring lamb, accompanied by a little of its sous-vide braised shoulder and tongue, a beautiful jus, roasted organic Jersey Royal potatoes, and a sauté of local baby spring vegetables, cooked by none other than Heston Blumenthal's former Fat Duck sous-chef Emily Watkins, something transformative happens. It goes like so: you taste it, realize that you cannot remember having eaten anything as good in a posh, stuffy, and far more expensive restaurant for a very long time, and then you look around at your convivial, relaxed surroundings and you think to yourself, "So who needs fine dining?" Every casual restaurant that opens and serves truly good food makes it that much harder for a fine-dining establishment to peddle food that is only slightly better at twice the price. And with so many casual restaurants of quality having opened in these recent recessionary years, it is hard not to think that fine dining has as a result been irretrievably marginalized to the realm of the special-occasion restaurant, as opposed to something for which we have time in our day-to-day lives.

Of all the chefs mentioned thus far in this book, David Hawksworth stands out for me as having reinvented himself and his product in such a way that fits perfectly with the contemporary mood. At Hawksworth Restaurant, at the Rosewood Hotel Georgia, the food is inventive but not nearly so complicated as what he did at West—and was never intended to be. It is still exceptionally good, with a great deal of finesse lurking discreetly behind the ostensibly simple presentations—a finesse, incidentally, that would not be there if he had not risen through the ranks of fine dining rather than doing the bistro circuit. A meal at Hawksworth remains a special event, but it is neither prohibitively expensive nor intimidatingly stuffy. Neither does it demand a great amount of the diner's time. The cooking does not ask, nineties-style, that you sit up and pay attention, and abort extant conversation in favour of discussing what is on the plate each time one lands on the table. And this seems to me to be the future of North American fine dining. For now, anyway—until the next rethink.

Across the rest of the country the simplification of fine dining was well in play. In Quebec, the revolution in product-sourcing that Normand Laprise worked so hard to set in place at Toqué! was ultimately so successful that by the end of the nineties Boileau venison and St-Canut pork and all their ilk were turning up at other, more casual restaurants all over the province. That is a measure of Laprise's legacy, but it also started to work against him, for what were once seen as Toqué! products could now be enjoyed in settings far less formal and expensive. So in early 2010, Laprise and his long-time business partner Christine Lamarche decided to lighten up the mood at Toqué! by adding a fourteen-seat bar that jutted out into the dining room, at which people could dine more casually, and adding a twenty-four-seat patio out front on Place Jean-Paul-Riopelle, and then, mindful of all the new thriving bistros selling simple food at far higher profit margins than theirs, set about conceptualizing one of their own. Brasserie T! opened on Rue Jeanne-Mance, in the shadow of Place des Arts in the entertainment district, early in the summer of 2010, and Laprise's quirky, imaginative, and unpretentious take on bistro classics has kept the forty-odd seats full pretty much ever since.

"It saved Toqué!" he told me over drinks there, late one evening in January 2012, of the resulting boost to his bottom line.

In Toronto, Susur Lee closed his eponymous Susur in the spring of 2008 and is now left with the casual Lee—where he once ventured into takeout, and now sells "cheeseburger spring rolls"—along with its waiting room, Lee Lounge. Sometime in the summer of 2012 he will open Bent, a venture with his two sons, Levi and Kai, on shabby-cool Dundas West. Lee had once feared Marc Thuet's restaurant next door enough to arrange for the police to be called to hassle their valet parking service on opening night. He once refused an air-conditioning repairman access to the ladder to their shared roof and Thuet's ailing compressors, and once in a staff meeting told his gathered employees that any one of them ever spotted eating bread purchased next door at Thuet would be summarily fired. But there was no need for the histrionics; Lee Lounge is the last one standing. Thuet's restaurant—which opened as Thuet Cuisine, then became Bistro and Bakery Thuet, then Bite Me, and finally Conviction, was shuttered in the autumn of 2010. Thuet now focuses entirely on his chain of bakeries, patisseries, and traiteurs, called Petite Thuet.

Squash and Mascarpone Ravioli with Truffle Butter

Chef Rob Feenie

Serves 4 as an appetizer

For the filling
1 butternut squash, about 1-1/2 lb (675 g), halved and seeded
1 tbsp (15 mL) fine extra virgin olive oil
Salt and white pepper
1/4 cup (60 mL) mascarpone
1/2 tsp (2 mL) nutmeg
2 tbsp (30 mL) grated Parmigiano-Reggiano

For the ravioli
1-1/2 cups (375 mL) all-purpose flour
4 large eggs
1 tbsp (15 mL) salt
Flour for dusting

For the sauce
1/4 cup (60 mL) rice vinegar
1/4 cup (60 mL) dry white wine
1 tsp (5 mL) 35% cream
1/2 cup (125 mL) cold butter, cubed
1 tbsp (15 mL) lemon juice
1/4 tsp (1 mL) white truffle oil
2 tbsp (30 mL) finely chopped black truffle (or an additional 1/4 tsp/1 mL truffle oil)
Salt
Fleur de sel

For the filling, preheat oven to 325°F (160°C). Brush the cut side of the squash with olive oil and season with salt and pepper. Place cut side down on a baking sheet lined with parchment paper. Bake until cooked through and soft—about 30 minutes. Set aside to cool. Scoop 2 cups (500 mL) of the flesh into a strainer lined with cheesecloth, place over a bowl, and leave to drain in the refrigerator overnight.

Transfer drained squash to a food processor and add the mascarpone and nutmeg. Blend until smooth. Press mixture through a fine-mesh sieve into a bowl, pushing it through with a wooden spoon or a spatula. Stir in the parmesan and adjust seasonings. Cover and refrigerate until ready to use.

For the ravioli, sift the flour into the bowl of a stand mixer equipped with the hook. Add 3 of the eggs, activate mixer at low speed, and add salt. Turn off the mixer when dough clumps together in a ball. If it feels sticky rather than tacky, incorporate a little more flour. Transfer dough to a floured work surface, knead for 2 or 3 minutes until smooth, and set aside to rest in the refrigerator for a minimum of 30 minutes. Dust dough with flour again before passing it through a pasta machine. Sprinkle with a little more flour if pasta sticks to the rollers. Continue passing dough through the machine until you attain a thickness of about 1/16 inch (1 mm). Cover with plastic wrap and rest for 30 minutes before using.

Sprinkle the inside of a ravioli mould lightly with flour, cover with a sheet of pasta, and gently press it into the form. Transfer the squash filling to a pastry bag equipped with a flat tip and then pipe about 1 tbsp (15 mL) into each ravioli mould. Lightly beat the remaining egg. Brush one side of a second sheet of pasta with the egg wash and then carefully place it egg side down over the filled ravioli. Gently press the pasta down around the seams, evacuating air pockets before sealing the edges. Roll over the surface gently with a floured rolling pin. Trim edges, then invert the mould onto a baking sheet lined with parchment paper. Transfer to the freezer. Continue until the supply of dough or filling is exhausted.

For the sauce, whisk the vinegar and wine together in a saucepan over medium heat, then reduce until the liquid becomes syrupy. Lower the heat, add the cream, and then whisk in the butter, incorporating it one piece at a time. Do not boil. Stir in lemon juice, truffle oil, and truffle. Add salt to taste, then set aside, keeping warm.

To finish, gently break apart frozen ravioli. Cook in batches in a large pot of boiling salted water until al dente—3 to 4 minutes. Remove with a slotted spoon, drain, and then arrange 5 to 10 ravioli on each of 4 warm plates. Spoon warm truffle sauce over ravioli and sprinkle with a little fleur de sel.

And Mark McEwan continues to thrive, but when he followed his fine food emporium, McEwan, with Fabbrica to add to his unmatched upscale portfolio of North 44, Bymark, and One, his new move was into casual Italian, complete with a Neapolitan pizza oven.

There are innumerable reasons why the next generation of chefs to open quality restaurants in Canada will never receive anything close to the level of media attention and general adulation as some of those I have touched on here. Primary among them is that the generation that is now winding down their cooking arrived in a relative vacuum. Montreal is an exception, for there, Laprise merely changed the local idea of haute cuisine, and steered the extant French model into a new Québécois identity built on local ingredients and a very local lack of pretension. But in Toronto, before Lee, Thuet, McEwan, and their ilk, there was virtually nothing. And Vancouver was in the same situation prior to chefs like Feenie and Hawksworth. So while today's young chefs have been raised with the entirely new expectation of fame through cooking, they are simultaneously poised for some rough luck. They are not going to get it. Because no matter how well they cook, or how inventive they are, they are not culinary revolutionaries but caretakers, carrying on and advancing good cooking traditions rather than showing them off for the first time as if they invented them. One does not get as much attention for that sort of thing, at least not from conventional, professional media.

But there is one exception: television, and in particular the often mystifying but incredibly pervasive influence of the Food Network and its shows like *Top Chef Canada*, the spinoff of the long-running American series that in Canada is co-hosted by Top Judge Mark McEwan. Late in the autumn of 2011, McEwan also hosted all three finalists from its highly successful first season for a special dinner at his financial district restaurant Bymark, where, under the aegis of the Visa Infinite dining series, they would all cook together, each contributing a course to a six-course meal (four of them, plus cheese and dessert). So I brought my mother down to check in on the next, TV-friendly generation, and we more or less agreed on the whole oeuvre. Top Chef finalist Rob Rossi, who has since opened a restaurant in Toronto's west end called Bestellen, prepared a first course of scallop crudo with arugula purée, Meyer lemon, smoked Maldon salt, and bottarga. It had pleasant flavours but desperately needed colour. Next up was Top Chef winner Dale MacKay, who succeeded Rob Feenie at Lumière and then, after it closed, opened Ensemble. His black cod with pork Thai broth, bok choi, smoked maitaki, coriander, and chili was flavoursome but busy, and as it had too much consommé to be a fish dish, and too much fish to be a soup dish, I was left somewhat confounded as to what it was really supposed to be. Then show finalist Connie DeSousa (and John Jackson, her co-chef and co-owner at the Charcut Roast House, in the Hôtel Le Germain in Calgary) sent out wooden boards loaded with grilled High Country bison heart kielbasa with grainy mustard and fennel-kraut. This was the showstopper. It was exactly what it said it was, and sublimely tasty to boot. Everyone at the shared tables was hacking at the sausages with abandon, tucking in to more and more of what was almost certainly their first buffalo heart.

Impressed, soon thereafter I followed the pair back to Calgary, where the two had met years earlier as young cooks at the Owl's Nest, one of those old-fashioned French restaurants of the sort in which high-end North American hotels used to specialize, where the tartare was chopped and the sole filleted tableside by a maître d' or captain in a polyester tux. In the interim both had worked stateside, largely in the San Francisco area, where DeSousa had done time at the venerable Chez Panisse and Jackson had served as the opening executive chef at the swanky St. Regis hotel, where he once again had DeSousa in his brigade. What Jackson and DeSousa and their spouses opened in 2009 in the Le Germain is as starkly opposed to the luxurious goals of the St. Regis as it is to the out-of-date faux Old World silliness of the Owl's Nest. It is utterly casual in every way. Plates are intended to be shared, and the food is rustic, unrefined, and brimming with flavour—just like that kielbasa. The first time I visited, I sat at the bar and ate an excellent house-made mortadella followed by a smoked turkey leg. On my second visit, I fell for Jackson and DeSousa's tuna preserve, served in a Mason jar with preserved lemon and potatoes, and her country sausage and rotisserie chicken. Meals there taste like what you would like to eat each weekend at the cottage but do not always quite get around to.

But as if Charcut were not casual enough for them, they soon announced plans for a pop-up restaurant to be held in Calgary in late January 2012. They were to be joined in the kitchen by the young Toronto chef whose charcuterie and timely affection for all things offal had once drawn so much attention to the Toronto restaurant The Black Hoof—Grant van Gameren. It had in fact originally been van Gameren's idea to have DeSousa and Jackson join him as guest chefs at The Hoof, but when he unexpectedly quit that restaurant late in the summer of 2011, they stood the plan on its head, and van Gameren found himself Calgary bound in a vicious cold snap. I decided to tag along too, tracking them all down to a semi-industrial wasteland of Calgary to 1A Street SW, where amidst the autobody repair shops and other industrial storefronts, I finally found a promisingly well-trodden path in the snow leading to a smoked-glass door marked "Charpop." It was minus twenty-nine, so I pushed it open eagerly. Inside what turned out to be a bakery, tables were pressed one up against another along a far wall. DeSousa was working over the stove in another corner, while Jackson was doing prep at a temporary table, van Gameren at another. A whole array of familiar faces from Charcut sporting Charpop T-shirts were spread out in between, chopping and slicing and wrapping up portions of things in cellophane and putting them aside for later in all the usual semi-orchestrated chaos of the pre-service rush. They were preparing for the third and final night of Charpop, and I asked Jackson how the first two had gone.

"We really wanted to start the year off doing something totally new—and we did!" he told me, with his customary enthusiasm and slightly mad grin. "To bring in someone of this calibre"—Jackson gestured at van Gameren—"and it's Calgary's first pop-up. And it's like a real restaurant—not just a dinner party. If you're going to do it, do it right, I say. It was hard—but it was fun."

The "real restaurant" part of the equation was as yet a long way from popping up, so I focused my attention on the cooking, and in particular checked in on van Gameren. He was slicing up a beef tongue for a sandwich he makes with brioche in place of the classic deli-issue rye. I noted with pleasure his heap of *boudins noirs* and the lobes of raw Quebec foie gras. I watched him heat a knife by plunging it into a large bowl of steaming-hot water, wipe it dry, and then set about cutting the double lobes of liver into thick slices—and without first separating them to remove the thick vein that holds them together.

"You should have the foie gras tonight," van Gameren advised me.

"Is the *boudin* going to end up on the same plate?" I asked hopefully. (It is an excellent combination.)

"Yes. With rutabaga purée and bourbon gastrique."

I was in.

"Grant's pretty popular out West. He's got a following," DeSousa volunteered, only half turned away from the octopus she was braising on the hob.

I looked over the menu to see what else van Gameren had on it that night. Smoked veal sweetbread, pig skin, white bean, escarole; cabbage and bone marrow soup; The Original Tongue on Brioche …

"I think everything we're doing here is doable at Charcut," DeSousa said.

"If you want the truth," van Gameren countered, softly, "Connie and John are outselling me here four to one."

DeSousa was now working on prepping a potato gratin, slicing small Yukon Golds from local grower Poplar Bluff and arranging them in individual cast-iron pots, then sprinkling a little crumbled Asiago on top, then some *guanciale*, and then flooding it all with some yogurt-thick 52 percent cream. Other dishes from the Charcut crew included beef heart steak with bannock, arugula, and ricotta salata; rabbit pie topped with shaved lardo; beef cheek with squash and savoury scone; and a *side* dish of open-faced croissant with lamb, sumac, nigella seeds, and mint.

It was already five o'clock and the first seating was due in less than two hours. Soon the prep tables were pushed back against the wall of ovens to make a temporary pass, and the servers unfolded other tables to throw together an impromptu dining room. Some early guests arrived, and were held at bay in the storage room out back. A local CBC-TV crew suddenly materialized, to interview kitchen staff and broadcast live as the first plates left the pass.

"You would never get any media attention for this in Toronto," Grant says to me, *sotto voce*.

Which is true (unless you count blogs and Tweets). But it would not have been true a decade ago. And a few hours later, as I finished his plate of foie gras and blood sausage and moved on to DeSousa and Jackson's beef heart steak, I was thinking contentedly about the not-so-distant future, when travelling Calgary chefs might get to make such disparaging remarks about their hosts in Saskatoon or St. John's. The country is getting to a good culinary place—but the journey does require a lot of pushing and pulling each other along.

In Toronto these days most of that action is happening at restaurants with forty seats or fewer—casual places like The Black Hoof (which is soldiering on without van Gameren) and others of that ilk, at which the cooking is simple, the emphasis is on the quality of ingredients, and the only daring on display is the enthusiastic deployment of offal, which still has novelty value here.

At the high end, life is far quieter. In fact, the chef behind the most ambitious plans for Canada this year is a U.S.-based Frenchman, orchestrating his moves from an office over a restaurant kitchen on East 65th Street in Manhattan. For, just fifteen months after shutting down Lumière and db Bistro Moderne in Vancouver, chef Daniel Boulud had launched another two-pronged assault on the Canadian market. He would start in Montreal, where at the end of May—just a tick before Grand Prix weekend—he opened Maison Boulud, in the venerable Ritz-Carlton, fresh from its $233-million makeover. Then, in a repeat display of reckless timing, he would open a Café Boulud in the completely new Four Seasons Hotel Yorkville right before the start of the Toronto International Film Festival. When I saw him in New York in the spring of 2012 he allowed that the timing of it all *was* a little crazy. I next caught up with him in Montreal, when I bumped into him wheeling a suitcase down Rue de la Montagne with a cell phone clapped to one ear. He was lost, looking for Loews Hotel Vogue. We were both in town for the same reason, but on different sides of the pass: that night would mark the first trial run of Maison Boulud at the not-yet-open Ritz-Carlton. Boulud made me promise to not write about it, or to give him a hard time. No need. Some of the dishes were subpar for him, but still better than they had any right to be on a pre-opening night. And a few others were perfect, and brought me right back to a recent meal at his flagship Restaurant Daniel, where I had dined alone, and spent a good part of the night muttering to myself, "How I miss fine dining, how." Boulud is welcome here; I eat it all.

ACKNOWLEDGMENTS

This book relied heavily on the unfailing goodwill of some of my favourite chefs, who were frequently called upon to be generous with their time, recipes, food, and hospitality in other forms (read wine cellars). So I must first thank, in no particular order, Mark McEwan, David Lee, Rob Gentile, Rob Feenie, Thomas Haas, Normand Laprise, Frank Pabst, Susur Lee, Yvan Lebrun, Connie DeSousa, John Jackson, David Castellan, and the inimitable Marc Thuet. Some of their business partners (sometimes wives) also stand out for special mention. Through her excellent and free-flowing wine pairings Biana Zorich personally saw to it that I never once had to waste valuable dining time reading a wine list at Bistro and Bakery Thuet, which I always appreciated. The long and discreet reach of Christine Lamarche ensures that every meal at Toqué! runs as smoothly as clockwork. The exceptionally gracious Rolande Leclerc does the same for Restaurant Initiale. Likewise, Yannick Bigourdan at Nota Bene. Annabel Hawksworth is especially good at reminding her husband, David, of the things he said he would do (like writing recipes), but more than that, I am grateful to her for arranging my visit to the West Coast Fishing Club in the Haida Gwaii, where I rediscovered a long-neglected love of fishing. My generous hosts there—and in particular Brian Grange—deserve special thanks. So do the two highly dedicated CEOs of two restaurant groups: Jack Evrensel at Top Table, and Richard Jaffray at Cactus Club Café group. My love and understanding of smoked meat would not exist were it not for the generous attention paid me by Johnny and Abie Haim. Getting around between all these places was made a lot less expensive thanks to the generosity of the tourism boards of British Columbia, Vancouver, Whistler, and Calgary. The Opus Hotel and Rosewood Hotel Georgia in Vancouver, along with the splendid Auberge Saint-Antoine in Quebec were always there for me with a lovely room when I needed a place to stay. My editors at *Maclean's* magazine—Ken Whyte, Dianne de Fenoyl, Dianna Symonds, and Mark Stevenson—were always game to send me places even when they knew that I had an ulterior motive of book research, which was very helpful indeed. And finally, I have to thank Andrea Magyar for her patience, support, and excellent editorial suggestions, as well as editor Shaun Oakey who helped make many things sound better and more accurate than the way I handed them in, and David Ross, who knocked it all into such good shape on the page.

Index